W9-CFL-395

Bottlenotes

Guide to
Wine

Around the
World in
80 Sips

*From Napa to Lebanon,
Explore the Vineyards of Today
with Your Preferences in Mind*

Alyssa Rapp, Founder and CEO,
Bottlenotes, Inc.

A **adams**media
Avon, Massachusetts

Contains material adapted and abridged from *The Everything®
Wine Book, 2nd Edition* by Barabra Nowak and Beverly
Wichman, Copyright © 2005, 1997, by F+W Publications, Inc.

Published by Adams Media, an F+W Publications Company
57 Littlefield Street
Avon, MA 02322
www.adamsmedia.com

ISBN-10: 1-59869-787-0
ISBN-13: 978-1-59869-787-2

Library of Congress Cataloging-in-Publication Data
is available from the publisher.

Printed in China.
J I H G F E D C B A

This publication is designed to provide accurate and authoritative
information with regard to the subject matter covered. It is sold
with the understanding that the publisher is not engaged in rendering legal, accounting, or other professional advice. If legal advice
or other expert assistance is required, the services of a competent
professional person should be sought.

> —From a *Declaration of Principles* jointly adopted
> by a Committee of the American Bar Association
> and a Committee of Publishers and Associations

Many of the designations used by manufacturers and sellers to
distinguish their product are claimed as trademarks. Where those
designations appear in this book and Adams Media was aware of
a trademark claim, the designations have been printed with initial
capital letters.

*This book is available at quantity discounts for bulk purchases.
For information, please call 1-800-289-0963.*

Contents ::::::::::::::::::::::::::::......

Part 2 Around the World in 80 Sips, from West to East • 115

Introduction

Like the discovery of wine itself, Bottlenotes began by accident, as the entrepreneurial story goes. Wine for me, like so many people, began as a hobby and a passion, intertwined with my love of travel. I spent the summer after my sophomore year of college working for an NGO in South Africa. There I formally toured my first wine region, Stellenbosch, in the Western Cape. A student of art history and politics as an undergraduate at Yale University, even during this first summer of my "wine life," wine, like art, served as a window into history, politics, cultures, and local cuisine, all of which fascinated me.

During the winter and spring of 1999, I lived in the Netherlands for six months and enjoyed traveling to France, Italy, Austria, Germany, and Spain. In each place, wine served as a socially organizing principle of meals and lifestyle in a way I had not previously experienced in the United States.

Upon my return to the United States (and passing the American milestone of one's twenty-first birthday), I began to enjoy wine as a hobby, both in restaurants and by touring some of our nation's great wine regions. My wine travel culminated in a twelve-week trip throughout New Zealand and Australia in the spring of 2003, where visits to wineries and the countries' various wine regions actually served as one of the themes of the journey. Thus the seeds of Bottlenotes as a concept—that of an ongoing tour

"Around the World in 80 Sips"—actually began quite literally through wine travels in Europe, the United States, and the Southern Hemisphere.

The Bottlenotes story formally begins when I was a first-year MBA candidate at Stanford University's Graduate School of Business. There I co-presided over a wine club with hundreds of members at Stanford Business School. I had the great fortune of dramatically expanding my wine knowledge via classmates from wine families and through frequent guest lectures from Napa Valley icons such as Jack Cakebread and Peter Mondavi, Jr., both Stanford alums who are Bottlenotes board members today. As I tasted more and more wine, I ran into a logistical problem: There was no easy way to electronically store the tasting notes I accrued. This problem served as the basis for the solution that Bottlenotes offers today in our online wine cellar (My Cellar) technology.

I also was so impressed by this community of wine enthusiasts coming together multiple times per week to taste wine that, à la Peter Pan, I simply did not want the learning to end. Starting a commercial wine club—one that mirrored the best wine clubs of Napa Valley but added the twist of personalization (a growing trend on the Internet as a whole)—seemed like a perfect resolution. So in the spring of 2005, when I married my wine passion and experiences with those of my business partner, Kim Donaldson, Bottlenotes was born.

We hope that you enjoy a brief overview of the knowledge that the fabulous Bottlenotes team and I have acquired over the past few years as presented in this book. Now we invite you to escape the pressures and demands of everyday life, uncork a bottle of wine, and join us on a brief journey "Around the World in 80 Sips!"

Acknowledgments

Having family and dear friends who are published authors and editors, I have long been aware that writing a book is far more than the work of a single writer. This fact could not be more true than in the case of *Bottlenotes Guide to Wine: Around the World in 80 Sips.*

Overt credit is owed to the following Bottlenotes interns and consultants who toiled for summers and throughout the academic years helping us research, prepare, and edit this material: Matt Inkeles, Michael Levinson, Antonia Moran, Drew Niles, Sam Tanzer, and most of all, to Sarah Orrick. "BottleBook" (as it's affectionately called in "BottleWorld") would not have been possible without Sarah's meaningful contribution.

To the rest of the Bottlenotes team, specifically to Ainsley, Bayard, Forrest, Katherine, Kim, and Sean: Bottlenotes as a whole would not be doable without your endless hard work and commitment, for which I am eternally grateful.

Great thanks is also owed to Chelsea King at Adams Media for her persistence in getting this deal done in the first place.

Without further ado, it's time to start the wine journey!

Part 1

What Wine Is All About

Before we start our travels "Around the World in 80 Sips," we must take the time to get to know the how, when, and why of wine first. In this section, we will take a look at the history of wine, how it is created, what the different types are, and which ones you might like. We will also give you the basic information on the various varietals. Long story short: By the end of Part 1, you will be equipped to start tasting and exploring the world of wine!

CHAPTER 1

Wine Throughout History

No one knows exactly how wine was discovered—in fact, it was probably an accident. Since wine is the natural result of fermented grapes, no one "invented" it. As people began to store produce, planning ahead for colder seasons, the grapes would have created wine on their own—albeit a far less sophisticated beverage than we enjoy today.

Wine Is Born by Accident in the Ancient World

Although historians have yet to fix an exact date for the widespread consumption of wine, we know it was most likely between 4000 and 6000 B.C., and potentially even earlier than that. Recent discoveries have indicated wine-making in China at this time, but Mesopotamia and Egypt (which mark the boundaries of the Fertile Crescent) are commonly regarded as its birthplace.

Wine figured prominently in Persian culture, which claimed the honor of its invention. One fable claimed that an ancient king hid his beloved grapes in an earthen jar labeled "poison." A discontented member of his harem attempted suicide by drinking from the jar, but instead of dying she found her spirits quite rejuvenated. After she shared the drink with her king, he not only took her into his favor but decreed that, henceforth, grapes would be allowed to ferment. As we all know, men have been buying women drinks ever since.

The first wine country, ancient Persia both toasted its gods and paid its employees with wine. (As the contributors to this book know, we at Bottlenotes have also leveraged this age-old compensation technique!)

Egyptians Develop New Ways to Cultivate Grapes

Although the ancient Persians were the first culture to make wine, the ancient Egyptians pioneered the use of techniques still employed today. In addition to developing arbors and pruning methods, they crushed and fermented grapes in large wooden vats. Mainly producing sweet white wine, most likely from the grape Muscat of Alexandria, the Egyptians used their product in funeral rites out of respect for their gods. The amount of wine used to anoint the deceased's body and belongings directly corresponded to his or her social status. The grape varieties the Persians used to make wine are believed to be the forbears of those we use today.

Wine Travels to Greece

The Phoenicians, who were situated between Egypt and Mesopotamia along the Fertile Crescent, spread wine throughout the Mediterranean during voyages to Greece, Sicily, and north-central Italy. The earliest written account of wine appears in the Old Testament of the Bible. In Genesis, Noah planted a vineyard after the Flood and made wine. After the first wine came the first occasion of drunkenness—and a lesson about moderation.

No Age Limit During Ancient Times

As absurd (or alcoholic) as it might sound today, wine and beer were the primary beverages consumed—even for children—because water was far more dangerous than wine (and tasted like vinegar with a hint of cider). Wine was the chosen drink of the upper class, while commoners mainly drank beer.

Greeks Democratize Wine

The Greeks embraced wine more enthusiastically than any culture before, and, in keeping with the tenets of democracy, all classes, not just the aristocrats, imbibed. Used in commerce, prescribed as medicine, and an essential component of religious rituals, wine was said to fill over half of the vessels used each day.

The Greeks considered it barbaric to drink wine on its own, so they diluted it in varying proportions with water and used herbs and spices to mask spoilage. Storing the wine in jugs sealed with pine resin added a unique flavor.

An important component of the economies of Greek cities, wine was traded within Greece and exported throughout the Mediterranean world. As the Greeks began to colonize the western Mediterranean, they brought their grapevines and winemaking technology along.

Romans Make More Advances

At its greatest outward expansion, the Roman Empire covered most of the Mediterranean as well as a portion of Europe. While the grapes predated the Romans in areas previously held by the Greeks and Phoenicians, the Romans loved wine and fostered its development throughout the empire. The Romans may also have been the first to store wine in glass vessels given that glass blowing emerged during this period as well.

Popularity Surge

By the first century A.D., Rome was awash with wine: Each person in the city of Rome drank, on average, half a liter per day. Winemaking techniques spread from Italy to Spain, Germany, England, and France, and those regions developed their own vineyards. The increase in wine (particularly in the colonies) led to the emergence of corner bars in cities such as Pompeii. Emperor Domitian even ordered the vineyards of France be uprooted to eliminate competition. Fortunately that order wasn't fully executed, and it was rescinded two centuries later. When the Roman Empire fell for good in A.D. 476, the great wine regions of Europe were replete with vines.

Medieval Monks Work to Perfect Wine in Europe

Wine and its extraordinary properties have long been associated with spirituality and religion. While most of the religions practiced in the eastern Mediterranean incorporated wine in their rituals, it was the spread of Christianity in the fourth century that ensured the survival of viticulture and winemaking after the collapse of the Roman Empire. Because wine was such an integral part of the celebration of the Eucharist, the monasteries and cathedrals that sprang up across Europe took up winemaking and amassed substantial vineyard properties. The monks—who had the education, the financial backing of the Catholic Church, and the requisite time for cultivating land and trying new techniques—became some of the most important winemakers of the Middle Ages.

Monastic wineries established extensive vineyards across Europe, particularly in Burgundy, Bordeaux, Champagne, the Loire Valley, and the Rhône Valley. During this time, France emerged as the preeminent winemaking region in the world.

Wine and War Don't Mix

In 1152 Henry II of England married France's Eleanor of Aquitaine, whose dowry included the vineyard areas of Bordeaux and neighboring Gascony. The light-red wine produced in that region became popular in England under the name *claret*. By 1350, the port city of Bordeaux was shipping one million cases of claret a year. Sporadic fighting between the kings of England and France—known as the Hundred Years' War (1337–1453)—put an end to England's access to her much-loved wine. Any ship transporting the wine faced piracy; protecting the ships became prohibitively expensive, leading England to look beyond western France for wine.

England's trading friendship with Portugal inspired the creation of Port. Since the journey by sea from Portugal to England often ruined wine, the shippers in Oporto began adding a couple of buckets of brandy to the wine to stabilize it to ensure its arrival in good condition. As they experimented, they tried adding the brandy earlier and earlier until they were adding it during fermentation. This wine became known as, quite appropriately, Porto—or Port.

Inventions Spur Change

Even though the Romans may have used blown-glass containers to serve wine, pottery and stoneware jugs were widely used until the seventeenth century and the advent of commercial glassmaking. The first glass bottles were onion shaped. They eventually evolved into cylindrical bottles that could be stacked horizontally.

Needless to say, there would be no sideways stacking without an effective bottle stopper. Enter the cork.

Originally corks were tapered so they could both fit a variety of bottles and be manually removed. However, with the production of mold-made bottles and horizontal stacking, the cylindrical cork we see today was developed for maximum wine containment. This type of cork, as we know, requires a special tool to open the bottle. Corkscrews of all kinds continue to be introduced to this day.

Reaching Out to the New World

As the Europeans discovered and colonized new lands, they brought certain aspects of the culture that shaped the areas they settled. One of these aspects, unsurprisingly, was wine, which spread to the Americas and South Africa in the 1500s and 1600s and to Australia in the 1700s. The history of European wine thus became intertwined with that of the New World.

New World, New Vines, Great Wines in the Americas

The wine-guzzling conquistadors who arrived in South and Central America from Spain in the 1500s were directly and indirectly responsible for introducing winemaking to those lands. After defeating Montezuma in 1521 and causing the collapse of the Aztec Empire, Hernando Cortéz (later the governor of Mexico) threw himself a party. Once he ran out of wine, he ordered all of the Spanish settlers to plant vines on their new property.

This action did not please the king of Spain, as he saw his colonies as a source of raw materials and a captive market for Spanish goods. He levied heavy taxes on the colonies and ordered the vineyards destroyed. The edict was enforced most aggressively in Mexico, abruptly ending the burgeoning wine industry there.

The church was the sole exception to the king's edict. As in Europe after the fall of the Roman Empire, the vineyards survived under the care of the church. Missions (predominantly Jesuit) were established in Chile, Argentina, Peru, and Mexico early on. A series of missions along the Pacific Coast would later bring winemaking to California.

Colonial Experiments in North America

Early settlers of North America brought a mighty thirst for wine. The first wine from grapes native to American soil was made in Jamestown in 1609, and it was not what the colonists were used to. Nor what they wanted.

The colonists' next step was to import vine cuttings (rootstock) of *Vitis vinifera* from Europe so they could grow more familiar varieties—Cabernet Sauvignon, Merlot, Chardonnay. They planted vines from every great European wine region along the Atlantic Coast. Even Thomas Jefferson, the wine geek of his era, planted vines at Monticello. Despite their enthusiasm, no one succeeded. Each vineyard would die off after only two or three years. Although no one was certain of the cause, the weather and indigenous diseases were most often blamed. A hundred years later, another possible cause came to light.

Even though the original vinifera vines failed, new American varieties emerged in the 1800s. No one knows for sure, but it is generally assumed that they were produced by chance through pollen exchange between the vinifera and earlier American varieties. These hybrids became the foundation for the wine industry in the eastern United States. Winemaking centers emerged in Ohio, Missouri, on the shores of Lake Erie, and in the Finger Lakes region of upstate New York. The American wine industry was on its way.

California Dreamin'

In approximately 1770, Franciscan monks began to establish missions—and plant vineyards—up the coast of what would become California. Father Junípero Serra led the way when he planted the first vineyard at Mission San Diego. He traveled north and established eight more missions, earning him the nickname the "father of California wine."

The gold rush of 1849 brought frenzied growth both in terms of population and vineyards. By this time Sonoma had 22,000 acres under vine, and Napa had 18,000. The Santa Clara Valley and Livermore Valley were widely planted and had numerous wineries as well. Many pioneer vintners settled south and east of the San Francisco Bay where most of the bottling plants were located. With the advent of the railroad, California wines became available in eastern markets and shipped around the world. By the end of the century, all of the state's winemaking regions were producing wine. California had become the premier wine-growing region in the United States.

An International Wine Crisis

In 1863, an unidentified vine disease was noticed in France's Rhône Valley. By 1865, the disease had spread to Provence. By the late 1860s, vine growers all over France were watching their vineyards die before their very eyes. Over the next twenty years the disease decimated nearly all the vineyards in Europe.

The scourge was called phylloxera, a louse indigenous to the eastern United States. While barely visible to the naked eye, the insect sucks the nutrients from the roots of grapevines and slowly starves the life out of the vines. Since Native American grapevines have a thick and tough root bark, they suffered no damage from the parasite. Tragically, vinifera vines had no such evolutionary protection.

The phylloxera spread, decimating vines in California, Australia, New Zealand, and South Africa. Eradicating phylloxera seemed hopeless until a solution emerged: Graft vinifera vines to the pest-resistant American rootstocks. Although it worked, it was a long and laborious undertaking to graft and replant each and every vine in Europe.

Prohibition Wipes Out an Industry

The winemaking business always has its ups and downs—sometimes due to insects and other times due to politics. In 1920, politics was the culprit of an industry-wide crash in the United States. The Eighteenth Amendment to the U.S. Constitution created Prohibition, criminalizing alcohol. The Prohibition movement in America was not a sudden phenomenon; it started county by county, state by state. Its long-term effects continue to impact the industry today. At the outbreak of World War I, thirty-three states had gone dry.

The Eighteenth Amendment was ratified on January 29, 1919, and one year later Prohibition began, making virtually all alcoholic beverages illegal. The Volstead Act, spearheaded by the Minnesota congressman of the same name, defined intoxicating liquors as any beverage containing more than one-half of 1 percent alcohol. Many supporters of the Eighteenth Amendment were dismayed as they had assumed that the "intoxicating liquors" to be banned were the high-alcohol distilled spirits with 40 percent alcohol—surely not beer with its 3 to 7 percent alcohol, or wine with its less than 15 percent alcohol.

Lasting Effects

Almost immediately, the American wine industry was decimated. Vineyards were uprooted, equipment was abandoned, and growers and producers had to find creative ways to stay in business. Cooking wine could still be produced as long as it was salted and undrinkable. Sacramental and religious wines were still allowed and somehow found their way to secular markets. Medicinal alcohol was legal, too, because it was not for beverage purposes. So doctors began prescribing more and more of it. Home producers were permitted to make up to two hundred gallons of wine a year. The overall effect of Prohibition was to annihilate a once-thriving industry.

By 1933, when the Twenty-first Amendment repealed Prohibition, great damage had already been done. The country had lost an entire generation of winemakers and wine drinkers. Other effects of this "noble experiment" last to this day, specifically regarding direct-shipping and distribution laws. By 1936, fifteen states had laws that created state monopolies on wine sales and prevented free-market competition. Other states, while allowing hotels and restaurants to serve wine, banned bars and "liquor by the drink." Other states left serving and selling options to local jurisdictions. The aftermath of Prohibition is a hodgepodge of laws that vary from state to state and community to community. The last effect is that shipping wine within America is like shipping wine to fifty different countries.

The Wine Boom in the United States

As the wine industry rebuilt itself after the repeal of Prohibition, it found a market much changed in its thirteen-year hiatus. The quality of wine was negatively impacted because California grape growers had to deliver grapes that shipped well rather than those optimal for winemaking. Wineries mostly sold their wines to wholesalers who bottled them under their own brands and then, in turn, sold them under generic names like "Chablis" and "Burgundy." In 1940, Americans were drinking one gallon of wine a year per person; the French were consuming forty gallons.

JFK and Julia Child Join Forces

The American wine boom really began with the affluence of the late 1950s. Wine was attractive to educated suburbanites, especially those wealthy enough to travel abroad. While most of the world considered it a delicious beverage, Americans began to see it as a status symbol.

A few role models helped. When John F. Kennedy came to the White House he brought his wife, Jackie, who loved all things French. French restaurants and French wines became very trendy. In addition, from a kitchen in a Boston television studio, Julia Child taught a generation of Americans how to prepare French cuisine—and how sipping and cooking can go together.

New products appeared in wine stores to meet the growing demand. Portuguese rosés hit the shelves. They were sweet, fruity, slightly fizzy, and imported from Europe. From West Germany came Liebfraumilch, a flowery, fruity, and slightly sweet blend of Riesling and other grape varieties.

Meanwhile, California's reputation for world-class wines rapidly grew. In the early 1970s, resourceful winemakers, many educated in their craft at the University of California at Davis, developed a new genre of California wine. In a blind tasting that pitted several California wines against top French wines in 1976, the American wines—Stags' Leap Cabernet and Château Montelena Chardonnay—won. This decision (by a panel of French judges), known as the Judgment of Paris, shocked and forever changed the wine world. Napa Valley was now on the global wine map.

Thirsty for Knowledge?

The 1976 Judgment of Paris was re-created for its thirtieth anniversary in 2006 with two panels in England and California. It was held in three stages. First they retasted the six California Cabs and four Bordeaux of the same vintages tasted in 1976. Next they tasted the same or similar wines in current vintages. The third stage featured samples of classic French Burgundies and California whites. The tastings took place simultaneously in two countries this time—England and in Napa Valley, California—and were connected through streaming video. For more information, visit www.decanter.com/news/80840.html.

Varietals Take Over

American winemakers began labeling their wines according to the grape variety they were made from, unlike European winemakers who identified their wines after the place where the grapes were produced. Instead of a glass of white wine with dinner, consumers knew to ask for a glass of Chardonnay.

Americans became attached to their new varietals: Cabernet Sauvignon, Merlot, Chardonnay, and Sauvignon Blanc. One California variety, however, was not having as much success in the 1970s: Zinfandel. Unfortunately, many growers had acre upon acre of Zinfandel vines whose grapes matured effortlessly in the California sunshine. The growers might have replanted their vineyards with other varieties had it not been for Bob Trinchero, owner of Sutter Home Winery, who was the first to make a fruity, pink, and slightly sweet rosé from this red wine grape. An instant and enormous success in the American market, the popularity of Sutter Home's White Zinfandel helped to drive annual wine consumption in the United States up from one to two gallons per person. Today, Dr. Jerry Seps, a formerly tenured history professor at Stanford University, makes what is regarded as the country's best, most elegant red Zin at the Storybook Mountain Vineyard.

The Last Twenty Years

Today every state in the Union has a winery. As wine-drinking Americans, we have upgraded our taste in wines, helped by the proliferation of wine classes, winetastings, dinners, wine publications, and tasting-note sharing platforms like Bottlenotes. While White Zinfandel remains a favorite for millions, there's a new enthusiasm for wine exploration. The White Zinfandel craze morphed into a Chardonnay trend that shifted to a Merlot fad. Now there are even newer fashions: Pinot Noir and Shiraz. It used to be that the popular wines of choice were the ones that people could pronounce. Now, brave wine drinkers dare to try Grüner Veltliner and Gewürztraminer.

California has taken to growing more Old World grapes. So-called Cal-Ital varieties like Barbera and Sangiovese are popular, as are the Rhône reds (made from Syrah, Grenache, and/or Mourvedre, traditional grapes of the Rhône Valley of France).

International collaboration as well as international competition has picked up. Famous names in wine—Mondavi, Lafite Rothschild, and Lapostolle—have invested heavily in land and facilities in places like South America to produce high-quality wines. On the other hand, Australian wineries have been able to give American producers a run for their money with well-made, inexpensive wines. They've been so successful that some U.S. wineries are labeling their bottles of Syrah with the Aussie name, Shiraz.

Technological Advances

Technology is ever advancing. Who would have thought just a few years ago that people would seriously be discussing screw tops in the same breath as fine wines? The fact is that tainted corks have spoiled too much good wine. So the seventeenth-century invention that has lasted for so long is beginning to be replaced more and more by synthetic corks made of plastic or glass and screwtops. Fear not, however: The romance of uncorking a fine bottle of wine will never be lost.

Consolidation in the wine industry—larger wineries buying up smaller ones—has also become a fact of life. It enables one producer to market many brands and gain shelf space in retail stores. For consumers, the positive effects of consolidation are lower prices and ease of purchase. But consolidation also has contributed to some negative effects for American consumers: consolidation of producers, coupled with the lock many distributors have on distribution in regional markets, creates limited choices for consumers in supermarkets and large retailers that stock only the well-known and highly promoted brands from large companies. With the proliferation of imported products in the United States, the Internet as a purchasing channel, and the growing number of educated wine drinkers like you, there will continue to be a market for quality wines. Keep reading for the tools to figure out which wine is right for you!

CHAPTER 2

Consider the Categories

From growing to bottling, there's a lot that goes into the production of each bottle of wine. For a winemaker, it's like you choose your own adventure—there are lots of options with a few dead ends. The more you know about how a wine is produced, the better you'll be at understanding nuances of taste.

Growing the Grapes: Viticulture 101

Many people in the know agree that the quality of the wine produced is the result of the quality of the grapes from which it was made. Grapes are very sensitive to the earth in which they are grown (the French term for which is *terroir*) and the weather patterns of the area (climate). As a result, one of the most important parts of growing grapes is the area in which they are planted. Unlike some produce, vines take extra effort since they require a trellis for optimal sun exposure. Viticulturalists have a wide range of trellises available, from the simple to the complex. The trellis directly affects the amount and quality of sun that the grapes receive. Vines awaken during the early spring and continue to grow throughout the summer, hopefully avoiding the development of rots or disease. Spring frosts can be detrimental, but enterprising farmers have discovered how to save their vines from freezing. Over the course of summer the grapes begin to ripen, developing the sugars that will eventually be converted into alcohol.

How Wine Is Made—Still Wines

Ever wonder how wine goes from grape form to liquid? Ever wonder what makes some wines red and some white? The process of making wine is quite involved. As a starting point, take a closer look at how still wines (wines without bubbles, non-sparkling, non-fortified) are made.

Harvest

Aside from those who subscribe to certain esoteric philosophies, most people regard the harvest of the grapes as the initial act in the process of winemaking. As with so many things in life, timing is everything. The length of hang time (the amount of time grapes spend on the vine) determines the maturity of the grape. Harvest too early and the grapes are acidic; harvest too late and they will be overly sweet. Since wine is the product of those grapes at the moment that they cease to mature, great wine can only come from grapes that have been harvested at the peak of their growth when sugar and acid levels are perfectly balanced. How that moment is defined is both a matter of science and of personal preference.

This critical decision depends upon more than the winemaker's palate. The weather plays a pivotal role in the ripening of wine grapes and their condition at the time of harvest. Ideally, the grapes are perfectly mature, dry, and clean; when excess moisture is in the atmosphere, grapes may develop fungal disease. Slightly fungal grapes can be left on the vine a few extra days if further ripening is needed. If rain is forecast, however, the fungus can become a larger problem, so the winemaker has little choice but to pick the slightly unripe grapes. This tradeoff holds true for healthy grapes as well: Winemakers must choose between an early harvest (safe yet with sometimes more mediocre results) or waiting to see if the following days are warm and dry (riskier though potentially fantastic).

The timing of the harvest is all the more complex in regions where temperatures vary throughout the day. For example, in warm climates, harvesting usually takes place at night or in the cool hours of the morning in order to deliver the grapes as fresh and cool as possible to the winery.

Not only will the final product be shaped by when the grapes are harvested, but how they were harvested also affects a wine. Despite the introduction of machine-related technology, the best wines, those that are crafted with an eye toward quality of product rather than cost of production, are made from grapes that are harvested by hand. Machines, though cost-effective, cannot pick whole bunches of grapes at once. Today's machines are neither as discriminating nor as gentle as human hands.

Preparing for Fermentation

After the harvest, the grapes are crushed to produce *must*, a steppingstone in the metamorphosis of grapes to wine. Although certain aspects of crushing vary by grape variety, the essential process is the same.

Today the vast majority of wineries use mechanical crushers (in place of human feet!) to release the juice from the grapes, though traditionalists still exist. Most white wine producers will remove the grapes from the stems, as the stems are liable to impart a harsh, undesirable taste in lighter white wines. In the production of some full-bodied whites, as well as many sparkling and sweet wines, whole bunches of grapes are crushed with the stems left intact.

Thirsty for Knowledge?

Interested in trying your hand at winemaking? While you might not get as hands-on (or feet-on) as Lucille Ball stomping grapes in *I Love Lucy*, there are a range of places you can get winemaking experience. Crushpad (www.crushpad.com) in San Francisco allows its consumer winemakers to join groups and virtually manage the winemaking process. The cost is typically $10,000 to $20,000 per barrel.

After the crush, the winemaker has a choice: to press the grapes for additional juice, risking increased astringency, or to begin fermentation immediately. The choice depends upon the grape variety and desired result. Red wines depend on skin contact for pigment and tannin and are therefore pressed after fermentation. White wines, on the other hand, become astringent when the juice is left in contact with the skins for too long. The method of press-ing is the decision of the winemaker. The more harshly the grapes are pressed, the less elegant the wine will be and vice versa. Presses have been developed to squeeze the grapes as gently as possible in order to keep the seeds, or pips, a great source of bitterness, from breaking and to avoid extracting bitterness from the skins.

In red wine production, the solids are pressed after the juice has fermented and the wine has been run off. The liquid extracted in this process can be used in the final blend.

The liquid at this juncture is often clouded with sedi-ment. Since clear juice ferments better than clouded juice, it is left to settle. Once the suspended particles have sunk to the bottom, the clear juice is run off into the fermentation tank. In order to keep the juice from fer-menting early, sulfur may be added and temperatures are kept low.

Fermentation

During fermentation, some wineries rely on ambient yeast cells to come into contact with the grape must nat-urally, yeast being the key catalyst of fermentation. Most modern wineries choose to control the environment more closely, adding their own strains of yeast in an enclosed tank. When yeast comes into contact with grape sugars, it converts the sugars into alcohol, heat, and carbon diox-ide. Higher sugar levels in the grapes at harvest usually yield wine with a higher percentage of alcohol in the fin-ished product. Because the reaction between the yeast and the grape sugars produces heat, it is important for winemakers to keep the temperature low to prevent the wine's flavor from boiling off.

Red and White Fermentation Differences

White wines are fermented in a closed tank to prevent oxidation and to keep the must from browning. Many

wines are fermented in small oak barrels, especially serious white wines. The exceptions are light-bodied, aromatic white wines. These are usually fermented in steel
tanks so that the oak will not overwhelm the grapes' natural fruit character.

Red wines are almost always fermented in oak barrels
but have their own protection as they are vinified with
the skins of the grapes. The skins rise to the top of the
tank and form a cap covering the surface area of the barrel. In order to soften the tannins, this cap usually inter-
acts with the must through one of several methods. Winemakers can either pump the must over the cap, which
is commonly referred to as "pumping over," or they can
physically punch down the cap into the must, referred
to as "punching the cap." While some wineries employ
machines for precision, the finest winemakers prefer
punching down by hand.

Aging

After fermentation a wine is left to age. The key factor impacting the aging of wine is the type of container
in which it is aged. Many wines spend some time in oak
barrels, whether big, small, old, new, American, Hungar-
ian, or French. Oak aging can last from a few months to
several years, depending, as always, on the varietal and
desired quality level. White wines can benefit from a
short period of aging in a barrel to extract a small amount
of oak flavor, while red wines often take a year or more.
Wines that are fermented in barrels are racked off the lees
(siphoned without the sediment that sinks to the bottom)
into a clean barrel for aging.

Occasionally a specific style will call for contact with
the lees, a process known as aging *sur lie*, or "on the
lees." Otherwise, wines that are separated from the lees
are aerated and clarified by this process, minimizing the
risk of developing unwanted odors. The majority of wine
is filtered in some manner to remove solid particles from

the wine. In addition, any remaining yeast particles are removed through this process, preventing the wine from refermenting and becoming bubbly.

Thirsty for Knowledge?

The thought of egg whites in wine may disgust you, but using egg whites as fining agents is actually quite common, especially in Bordeaux. Fining is the process in which egg whites (or gelatin, casein, bentonite, and a variety of other enzymes) are whipped into a barrel (three or four in a 25-gallon barrel) where they float through the barrel of wine, capturing particles as they float down, thus "fining" the wine. Fining comes after blending but before filtration and bottling in the winemaking process; it is performed to create more translucent wines and to improve color, odor, flavor, and stability. Egg whites are used in red wine for their capacity to reduce harsh tannins, and some winemakers believe that doing so gives the wine a certain silkiness that it would otherwise not possess. Separating the eggs for fining is stereotypically the role of the matriarch in a family, that is, unless egg whites by Costco are available.

Red Wine

The term *red wine* refers to all red wines, ranging in color from brick to deep purple. Made from grapes that are closer in appearance to black than red, the wine receives its color from the skins of the grapes, which are left in the barrel during fermentation. The color seeps from the skins and taints the clear juice, creating the recognizable color. The length of time the skins are in contact with the juice does more than determine color—it also affects the amount of tannins that are in the wine.

What's All the Talk about Tannin?

Tannin is found in the skins, seeds, and stems of grapes—as well as in the oak used in oak barrels for fermentation. Tannin imparts a "gritty" character into the taste in wine, "grit" that mellows with age, over time. Tannin imparts backbone and structure, thus ageability, to a wine. Tannin from seeds and stems are the most bitter, therefore least desirable, in wines, whereas tannin in skins and oak barrels is often consciously sought after. Red wine grapes with thinner skins that are often lighter in color (aka: Pinot Noir) tend to be "lower" in tannin, whereas red wine grapes that have thicker skins and are darker in color tend to yield wines with higher tannins (Cabernet Sauvignon, Petit Sirah). As oak barrels go, American oak tends to be the harshest, yielding the most "pronounced" tannins in wine, while French oak barrels often impact the most sinewy, elegant tannins in a wine. No matter whether the tannin comes from the grapes or the barrels, tannins in wine universally mellow over time.

There are many different styles of red wine, given the multitude of grapes and terroir that produce it, and often a single wine will encapsulate a few of these. Bottlenotes prefers to sort these by flavor and taste profile, as the taste is your primary experience with the wine! Bottlenotes separates red wine into the following flavor categories, which will be expounded upon throughout the rest of this book: *big and powerful*, *spicy*, *jammy*, *earthy*, *smooth and elegant*, and *fresh and fruity*.

Red wines are more powerful than whites. You don't want to drink red wine as cold as you drink white, but you don't want it hot, either. A cooked red wine, one that has been overheated, loses all of the pleasant aspects the wine might have had. There's a saying in the wine business that Americans drink their white wines too cool but their red wines too warm.

White Wine

The term *white wine* refers to still (table) wines that are not red or pink, though they may not be necessarily white. Most often a pale or golden yellow, white wines are normally made from similarly colored grapes such as Chardonnay or Pinot Grigio. White wines can also be made from red grapes that undergo a different process of obtaining the must. Although red grapes normally produce red wine, it is the skins, not the juice, that supply a wine's color. To create a white wine from red grapes, there are two options, both of which require the immediate removal of the skins. The juice might be crushed out of the grapes (most common), or the grapes might be pressed so that the juice and pulp shoot out of the skins (less common, except for certain sparkling wines). Regardless, both of these processes for making white wine from red grapes are the exception, not the rule, in white wine production. In short, most white wines are made from white grapes.

Although there are many different ways of categorizing whites, we at Bottlenotes think about white wine in terms of taste profile, as we do reds, as reflected by our white wine taxonomy: *full and lush*, *floral and aromatic*, *tangy and zesty*, and *crisp and light*. While these tastes come from different grapes, they are also affected by the different tools that winemakers may choose to employ. For a tangy and zesty wine, the grapes will often age in stainless steel tanks or in used, as opposed to new, oak barrels. For a more rich and buttery wine, a winemaker might employ malolactic fermentation. (Malolactic fermentation is the process of turning malolactic acid into *lactic* acid during the fermentation of wine. Lactic acid, à la lactose, imparts a creamy character to a wine.) Such white wines, stereotypically Napa Valley Chardonnays, can also stand up to newer French oak barrels for aging. Characteristics such as floral and aromatic often result from the indigenous grape variety itself (such as Pinot Grigio or Viognier). Crisp and light white wines offer the mildest of flavor profiles, characterized both by the winemaking style and by the grape variety utilized.

White wines can be consumed in nearly any situation—both before and during dinner—as they are light enough to be enjoyed without food, though they complement many different types of food quite well. Many experts believe that, contrary to conventional wisdom, white wine, not red, makes for the optimal cheese pairing at the end of a meal.

Rosé Wine

Rosés are often thought of as overly sweet, but a good rosé will have enough structure and acidity to go perfectly well with vegetables and protein prepared on the barbecue. Rosés are made in one of two ways. The best rosés are produced in the saigné method (*saigner* in French means "to bleed"), whereby red grapes are left in contact with the skins for just enough time to attract some pigmentation from the skins. Lesser-quality still rosés, or even high-end sparkling rosés, are made by blending red and white juice (red plus white equals pink).

Sparkling Wine

While sparkling wines are made nearly everywhere, *Champagne* refers only to those sparkling wines made in the specific region of Champagne, France. The vinification of sparkling wines in Champagne is strictly controlled, and specific techniques are required by law. The wines labeled as *méthode champenoise* or *méthode traditionelle* (traditional method) are made in the Champagne tradition.

There are several ways to make wine sparkle. The three main methods are: the traditional method; the transfer method; and the Charmat, or tank, method.

Each of the three processes begins with a still wine. These wines most often come from the grapes of Chardonnay, Pinot Noir, and Pinot Meunier vines, and the vintages need not be the same. Those labeled blanc de blanc are composed of only white grapes, like Chardonnay, and the blanc de noirs are made from red wine grapes.

Where Does That Sparkle Come From?

When still wines are blended into a cuvée, or a specific batch, additional sugars and yeasts are added for a second fermentation that creates the sparkle. This secondary fermentation occurs within the bottle itself!

Once the base wines are blended (*assemblage*, in French), the second fermentation begins. The most important step in the whole process, it is the only way to produce a fully sparkling wine. At this point, a mixture of still wine, sugar, yeast, and a clarifying agent, called the *liqueur de tirage*, or bottling liquor, is added to the final cuvée. The wine is then bottled with a temporary, beer-bottle–like crown cap. The added sugar and yeast react with one another, creating a second fermentation inside the bottle. As the sugar is converted into alcohol, the remaining carbon dioxide is trapped inside the bottle, infusing the wine with bubbles.

At this stage, the wine is far from finished. There still remains used yeasty sediment inside the bottles. The wines are now brought to a cellar where they will age for some time on their lees.

Machines Come in Handy

Traditionally the wines are placed on racks called *pupitres*. A *pupitre* consists of two heavy boards that are connected by a hinge. Each of the boards has sixty holes that are cut so that a bottle can rest, by the neck, in any position between horizontal and vertical. At first the bottles lie horizontally, and gradually, through a process called *remuage*, they are hand "riddled." This tedious process involves the rotation of each individual bottle, tilted very slightly over time, to loosen the yeast and allow it to settle into the neck of the bottle. Today, machines with computerized pallets (gyropalettes) have been designed to perform in days what takes around eight weeks to do by hand in the traditional manner. First developed by producers of Spanish Cava, these gyropalettes can riddle large quantities of bottles at once and increasingly are used worldwide.

After *remuage*, the bottles are aged *sur pont*—in the vertical, upside-down position—for anywhere between fifteen to thirty months, or even longer. Some high-quality wines can even benefit from aging this way for ten years!

Once the sparkling wines are finished aging, the wine is clear and all of the sediment is in the neck of the upside-down bottle. To remove the sediment, the necks of the bottles are immersed in a bath of freezing brine and the caps are opened. As the caps come off, the frozen sediment shoots out of the bottle, leaving a clear sparkling wine with a bit of space at the top. This is referred to in French as *dégorgement*, or disgorging. After the yeasty sediment is removed, the wines are topped off with a mixture of wine and a small amount of sugar to balance the high levels of acidity. This liquid is called the *liqueur d'expédition* (or "dosage"), and its sugar content varies depending on the wine's age and style. For an extra brut sparkling wine, no sugar is added. Increasing amounts of sugar, however, are added for brut, extra sec (medium dry), sec (medium sweet), demi-sec (sweet), and doux (very sweet) Champagne.

Finally, the wines are corked and a wire cage is fixed to the neck of the bottle to secure the cork. Champagne's vivacious acidity is a key factor in its tremendous aging potential.

Fortified/Dessert Wine

Dessert wines are those that have more than the legal limit of alcohol for table wines. In some cases the grapes have been left on the vine far longer than normal, allowing greater amounts of sugars to develop. In other cases it is because additional alcohol has been added after fermentation. The descriptor *dessert* comes from the U.S. custom of drinking these types of wines after dinner and because the wines are often sweet. The term *fortified*, referring to the excess of alcohol, is the most precise term used to describe the same type of wine. The three main types of dessert wines are late harvest, Port, and Sherry.

Late harvest wines are expensive and difficult to produce for several reasons. The longer the grapes are exposed to the weather, the more likely it is that adverse weather conditions will affect the grapes. The grapes that are used to produce these wines are quite shriveled and difficult to press, ferment, and clarify. These can be created through grapes that have been affected by the mold *Botrytis cinerea* (also known as "noble rot"), which concentrates and sweetens the grape, or frozen grapes (produced in northern areas) where the cold does much the same.

Sherry and Port both originate from the Iberian Peninsula (modern-day Spain and Portugal). Port wines (and those made in a similar style) are red wines that have had brandy added during the fermentation process. Originally added to stabilize the wine for travel, Port has developed into a distinct style of wine. Sherry is oxidized on purpose and contains a higher amount of alcohol than a normal wine. Since the aroma of an oxidized, or spoilt wine, is quite similar to that of Sherry, Sherry is delicious when done well but not for the faint of heart . . . or the mild of taste!

Kosher Wine

Many of the wines produced in Israel today are labeled as kosher, especially those from the larger wineries. This title indicates a fairly complex set of rules governing viticulture. For a wine to deserve the label, the vines must be at least four years old and left unharvested every seventh year (a Sabbath year for the vines/winery). Tools used during winemaking must also be in accordance with kosher practices and may not be used for purposes outside of winemaking. In addition, these tools may only be used by practicing male Jews. Often 1 percent of the finished product is poured out as a symbolic ritual. Kosher winemaking in no way negatively affects the quality of wine produced; some truly world-class kosher wines are now being produced in Israel, in particular those from Dalton Winery.

Thirsty for Knowledge?

The tradition of letting the winemaking staff rest every seven years—a Sabbath for the winemaking team—is still practiced in Israel today. In fact, that seventh year is taking place in 2008! Many modern wineries get around the required year of rest by having non-Jewish employees tend the vineyards. However, for a kosher wine to maintain its Meshuval (holy) status, the grapes and the wine can only be touched by Orthodox Jews throughout the winemaking process. Non-Orthodox winemakers interested in making kosher wine therefore must have a team of assistants whom they guide.

Organic and Biodynamic Wine

Organic winemaking, as with food, describes a specific method of farming, one that governs the use of chemicals in the process of cultivation. Organic wines are both farmed organically and made organically—without any preservatives, even sulfur, the most common stabilizer added to wine. The lack of sulfites often makes the wine taste predecanted when uncorked, which is always nice. The lack of sulfites also increases the probability of getting a corked (oxidized) bottle of wine, since sulfites help in stabilizing the wine and in ageability.

Although it sounds easy to make an organic wine, it is far more difficult to protect and fertilize the crop without the help of chemicals, and it is very expensive to do so. In addition, certain vineyards require a lot of intervention in order to optimize the quality of the grapes.

Sustainable farming is growing in popularity, as it requires the fewest amount of chemicals possible but allows their use if necessary. As a result, vineyards are healthier and produce better grapes, but the winemaker faces far less risk. Sustainable farms are often organic as well. It requires an enormous investment to make the transition to sustainable or organic farming, but many wineries in the Napa Valley are transitioning to this type of farming for the benefit of their land, even if they do not plan to market their wines as organically made.

Biodynamic wines are created in accordance with the earth's movements. Following the lunar calendar, biodynamic adherents will make their decisions about the grapes based on the phases of the moon. Some of the more interesting facets include rituals that may, to some, appear more religious than practical, such as burying a cow horn full of manure then digging it up and spraying it on the field, or fermenting oak bark in a domesticated animal's skull. Biodynamic winemakers are often prone to experimentation, and it's no question that the greater attention paid to the soil and the fewer chemicals applied to the soil, the better the wine.

Although farming sustainably, organically, or biodynamically may create challenges for the winegrower, these practices often positively affect the final product. Are the great lengths to which winemakers go in adhering to these farming practices effective? Ask your palate!

CHAPTER 3 ::::::::::::::::::::::

What's Your Type?

Ever notice how some of your friends always order Chardonnay while others order Sauvignon Blanc, or how some can't live without their Pinot and others their cult California Cabs? There is no doubt that many wine decisions are made by the tastes of one's parents or friends, what's most or least expensive on a given menu, which wine has the prettiest label, and what has the best commercial rating.

Wine Drinking Types

Taste in wine, as is true for taste in color, art, cuisine, and music, is highly personal. What governs your taste in wine is a compilation of what you see your parents and friends drinking, how much of your disposable income you spend tasting and exploring your wine preferences, and how swayed you are by commercial wine publications. Personal tastes are naturally influenced by where you have traveled, what types of cuisine you consume on a regular basis, and by what your friends drink.

Your taste in wine is also highly personal because it is influenced by your sensitivity to bitterness. Your sensitivity to bitterness is often disclosed by how you take your coffee or tea, or to the extent you salt your food. (For a complete elucidation, see later in this chapter: Why Wine Tastes Good: The Physiology of Taste.) In short, as is the case with so many things in life, your wine preferences are determined by your life experience, level of wine education, and personal biochemistry. Your tastes are highly personal, and ultimately you know what's right for you.

Bottlenotes System to Determine Taste Preference

In the land of Bottlenotes, we have categorized the types of wine drinkers as follows:

Luscious Crushers: Those most sensitive to bitterness, they often enjoy full and lush and floral and aromatic white wines, and smooth or jammy red wines.

Bold and the Beautiful: These are the tasters who are least sensitive to bitterness, who can drink the most tart, tangy, and zesty white wines, and the most bold, tannic, earthy red wines.

Those Who Love the Taste Tango, also known as Versatile Vinos: Of course, there are wine enthusiasts who can't get enough of that barnyard or manure character in their wines (Côtes du Rhône lovers), people who also often love highly spicy New World wines (Syrah/ Shiraz) or the earthy yet elegant Tempranillos from Spain. These tasters tango between the most intensely flavored wines, no matter their geographic origin. Some consider this group the supertasters of the wine world, those who either due to vast experience or their unique biochemistry find the merits in all types and styles of wine and who simply cannot be put in one bucket.

Bodacious Bouvenderies: These wine enthusiasts love to taste everything as they are still exploring what's right for them. Bottlenotes can help you if you fall into this category (or any of the others)!

Are you a Luscious Crusher, one of the Bold and the Beautiful, someone who loves to Taste Tango, or a Bodacious Bouvenderie? Take the test on page 39 or go to the Bottlenotes Web site (*www.bottlenotes.com*) and click on the *Personal Taste Profile* button. Input your answers and get wine recommendations tailored to your personal tastes, and see how others have answered the questions!

Do Critics Know Best?

No matter what type of wine drinker you are, there is one thing that is decisively true: The person who knows best what you will like is you. Although many wine publications might try to tell you otherwise, the truth is that in wine, as in so many things, you know what's right for you.

Robert Parker: Does He Know You Better Than You Do?

Back in the 1970s, an extraordinary man by the name of Robert Parker entered the world of wine. According to his own palate, he rated the world's most jammy, fruit-driven, thus often highly alcoholic, wines as the best. For this, I of course do not fault him; Robert Parker is entitled to his own personal taste as much as any of us! Unfortunately, we in the United States live in a celebrity-worshipping culture, one also not as historically steeped in wine as Europe. Although wine emerged in the United States as a major agricultural category in the nineteenth century, it was after we proved triumphant in that iconic 1976 Parisian winetasting that consumers started to catch on. As the wine industry as a whole took off in our great country, there was a void to fill of an arbiter as to what was good or bad wine. Robert Parker filled that void.

Robert Parker's power over consumer purchases in the United States, in conjunction with the ratings printed by the *Wine Spectator* (one of the most influential wine-rating magazines, along with Parker's *The Wine Advocate*), is unparalleled. An endorsement by Robert Parker and a rating of over 90 points in the *Wine Spectator* can make or break an entire vintage, let alone a winery or specific grape variety. Thus an internationalization of wine style is now commonly discussed: wines made anywhere in the world to please the palates of Mr. Parker and the reviewers at the *Wine Spectator*. This inspires winemakers to ignore or massage the more indigenous characteristics of climate or terroir to do so. The question is: How far will the industry go in the spirit of commercialization versus authenticity?

What's my take on all of this? As the CEO of a start-up enterprise in the great United States of America, I am as much of a believer in free-market economic principles as anyone. I am aware of the fact that there is a market for wines of Mr. Parker's preferred styles, or the wines wouldn't continue to sell. My concern is that demand in this case is not being determined by which types of wines consumers will truly enjoy the most. Instead, since wine is an extremely intimidating product, especially for the new enthusiast, we look to people or critiques to know "what's good" in order to know what to try, how to impress our clients or colleagues with our ability to identify that "show-pony" vintage or brand at a sell-dinner. What motivates Team Bottlenotes, and our phenomenal importers and domestic winery partners, is the possibility of the democratization of the wine world. We envision a marketplace where wineries are rewarded for high-touch, high-quality products, and where consumers are empowered to make purchasing decisions based upon what they like or what their friends with similar tastes recommend versus what any man or woman tasting wines in an office in New York City with white walls who wouldn't know you from Daisy.

There are, of course, an enormous number of people whose preferences are akin to those of Robert Parker. Those Luscious Crushers, as they are known in the Bottlenotes world, are a distinct segment of the tasting population, and they should be looking to Robert Parker for recommendations of what to try.

But how do you know what type of wine drinker you are? And if you should be looking to Robert Parker for your recommendations, or perhaps your new best friend on Facebook named Wendy Winemaker who lives in Walla Walla in a Winnebago or at the Waldorf? Keep reading.

Why Wine Tastes Good: The Physiology of Taste

"Taste is highly personal." I begin every educational tasting with these four words. Your taste in wine is influenced by both psychological and biochemical phenomena.

On the psychological side there are a range of influences. Your favorite foods as a child impact what you think you will enjoy as an adult; the type of wine your parents or spouse drink at home naturally influences your exposure to wine, thus your preferences. Similarly, how those same people take their coffee or tea impact your perceived sensitivity to bitterness. Where you have traveled, whether your group of friends are serious wine enthusiasts, your exposure to different countries, cultures, and cuisines—all of these factors impact your perception of your tastes. Perception of reality, as the cliché goes, can be as powerful as the reality itself.

While your preferences are influenced by these sociological factors, they are also influenced by your unique biochemistry. According to a study done at the University of California at Davis, one key proxy for the biochemistry of your mouth ia your sensitivity to bitterness.

What Does Being a Lemon Lover Have to Do with Anything?

If as a child you enjoyed sucking on lemons or lemon drop candies, or making and eating key lime pie, like me, it is no surprise that as an adult you enjoy a zippy Sauvignon Blanc or Sancerre (Sauvignon Blanc from France). Why? Because by virtue of enjoying those supertart treats there is a high likelihood that you are less sensitive to bitterness than others. That lack of bitterness sensitivity allows you to tolerate wines that are more tart, often accompanied by racier acidity, than someone who is more sensitive to bitterness. Other litmus tests of whether you are insensitive to bitterness include if you prefer dark to milk chocolate, if you take your coffee or tea black, and if you highly salt your food.

If you are less sensitive to bitterness, you will not only likely prefer the tangy and zesty white wines, but you will also enjoy earthy and big and powerful red wines.

At the other end of the spectrum, if you have a huge sweet tooth, pour milk and sugar into your hot beverages, and/or don't need a great deal of salt on your food to taste it, you might be more sensitive to bitterness. Bitter-sensitive wine drinkers typically prefer crisp and light or full and lush wines to the tangy and zesty whites. They also prefer smooth and elegant or jammy reds over others that are more earthy, spicy, or big and powerful.

Tongue-Tied

Diving even more deeply into the physiology of taste, the tongue itself and the number of taste receptors on your tongue impact your ability to taste wine and any other food and beverages for that matter. While the tongue was once believed to be separated into taste sections, with bitter in the back, sweet in the front, and salty/sour on the sides, it's been suggested that the entire tongue experiences each taste. Instead, the intensity with which one tastes anything is most greatly impacted by the sheer number of taste buds on the tongue. Those individuals with extraordinary amounts of taste buds are called supertasters. Supertasters have a heightened sense of taste as compared to the average wine taster, which may help them to distinguish a contemporary Napa Cabernet from a great Bordeaux from the 1970s, but whether or not you have this physical talent shouldn't keep you up at night.

Whether we are talking about taste at the broadest level and which models for taste you mimic (we all do, have no fear) from your friends or family, or at a granular level in terms of how many taste buds you have, it is positively indisputable that the more wine that you taste, the better you are at understanding what you like.

Thirsty for Knowledge?

Tim Hanni, the first Master of Wine in the United States, is the pioneer on the topics of taste buds, taste psychology, and taste preferences. He is revolutionizing the way chefs, wine experts, and consumers think about wine through his vast scientific partnerships and research on how people may experience wine completely differently due to the number of taste buds they have. Tim and his team have created a Budometer that tests your taste buds. He envisions a world where everyone will get their "buds done" to learn their taste sensitivity, making it easier to confidently explore and discover new wines. Bottlenotes would be thrilled to have this revolution happen! To learn more, go to *http://budometer.com.*

Bottlenotes' Personal Taste Profile: What's Right for You?

Bottlenotes devised a Personal Taste Profile, one that asks explicit questions about your taste preferences ("How much do you like wine of these varying styles?") and asks implicit questions about your taste preferences ("How do you take your coffee or tea?"). We combine your answers to the explicit and implicit questions to deduce your Personal Taste Profile. The actual questionnaire follows.

To complete the profile and receive real-time wine recommendations according to your personal taste preferences, all you need to do is go to **www.bottlenotes.com**, register, and you'll immediately be prompted to complete the Personal Taste Profile!

1. Which types of wine do you prefer to drink?
- ○ 1. White ONLY
- ○ 2. Red ONLY
- ○ 3. White, Red, Pink... all

2. White Flavor Profiles

(Please rank how much you like each flavor profile for WHITE wine on a scale of 1–5, where 1= not much, 5 = I love it.)

	1	2	3	4	5	no idea!
Crispy, Light, Delicate (Ex. Pinot Grigio)	○	○	○	○	○	○
Tangy, Zesty (Ex. Sauvignon Blanc)	○	○	○	○	○	○
Floral, Aromatic (Ex. Viognier, Riesling)	○	○	○	○	○	○
Full, Lush (Ex. Chardonnay)	○	○	○	○	○	○
Sweet (Ex. Sauternes)	○	○	○	○	○	○

not much⟶I love it

3. Red Flavor Profiles

(Please rank how much you like each flavor profile for RED wine on a scale of 1–5, where 1= not much, 5 = I love it.)

	1	2	3	4	5	no idea!
Fresh, Fruity (Ex. Merlot)	○	○	○	○	○	○
Smooth, Elegant (Ex. Pinot Noir)	○	○	○	○	○	○
Earthy (Ex. Bordeaux)	○	○	○	○	○	○
Jammy (Ex. Zinfandel)	○	○	○	○	○	○
Spicy (Ex. Syrah, Tempranillo)	○	○	○	○	○	○
Big, Powerful (Ex. Cabernet Sauvignon)	○	○	○	○	○	○

not much⟶I love it

4. **How adventuresome are you willing to be with respect to the wines you try?**
   - ○ 1. Very adventuresome
   - ○ 2. Kind of adventuresome
   - ○ 3. Once in a while I try new types of wines.
   - ○ 4. I'd like to stick to what's within the realm of tastes I know I like.

5. **From which general regions do you drink the most wine?** (Please rank them in order of importance 1=low, 5=high.)

	1	2	3	4	5	no idea!
1. North America	○	○	○	○	○	○
2. South America	○	○	○	○	○	○
3. Europe	○	○	○	○	○	○
4. (South) Africa	○	○	○	○	○	○
5. Australia/New Zealand	○	○	○	○	○	○

6. **Please choose which best describes you:**
   - ○ 1. I drink wine in social settings.
   - ○ 2. Wine is a part of my daily life.
   - ○ 3. I am a wine collector.
   - ○ 4. All of the above.
   - ○ 5. None of the above.

7. **How do you take your coffee or tea?**
   - ○ 1. Straight up.
   - ○ 2. With lots of cream.
   - ○ 3. With lots of sugar.
   - ○ 4. With cream and sugar.
   - ○ 5. I don't drink coffee or tea.

8. **How much of a sweet tooth do you have?**
   - ○ 1. None at all.
   - ○ 2. I eat sweets sometimes.
   - ○ 3. I can't live without my sugar fix.

9. **How much do you salt your food?**
   - ○ 1. Not at all
   - ○ 2. Sometimes
   - ○ 3. Always

10. **What is your favorite type of food?**
    - ○ 1. Italian
    - ○ 2. Indian
    - ○ 3. French
    - ○ 4. Thai or Chinese
    - ○ 5. Japanese
    - ○ 6. All American
    - ○ 7. Mexican or Spanish
    - ○ 8. Pacific Rim

Bottlenotes' Taxonomy of the World of Wine by Style

If you've completed the Personal Taste Profile and now are left wondering what it all means, check out the Web site. In the meantime, the following list details what kind of wines you might like depending on your taste preferences. Everyone is different, but here are some of our top recommendations! Enjoy.

WHITE WINES

Crisp and Light
> Chenin Blanc, Greco di Tuffo, Pinot Grigio

Tangy and Zesty
> Sauvignon Blanc, Sancerre (Sauvignon Blanc), Albariño, Malvasia Bianca

Full and Lush
> Chardonnay, Chablis (White Burgundy, also known as Chardonnay from the Burgundy region of France), Rousanne/Mersault

Floral and Aromatic
> Viognier, Gewürztraminer, Grüner Veltliner, Muscat

RED WINES

Fresh and Fruity
Pinot Noir (Californian), Merlot (California), Gamay

Smooth and Elegant
Red Burgundy (Pinot Noir), Merlot (French),
Brunello (Italy)

Big and Powerful
Cabernet Sauvignon (California), Nebbiolo (Barolos from Italy), Petit Sirah

Earthy
Sangiovese (Chianti), Pinotage, Côtes du Rhône,
red Bordeaux

Jammy
Zinfandel, Primitivo, Aglianico, Shiraz (Australia),
Pinot Noir (Central Coast, California)

Spicy
Syrah, Grenache, Mouvedre, Carminere, Tempranillo

ROSÉ WINES

Full, fresh fruit
Rosés of Syrah, Zinfandel, or Cabernet Sauvignon
(often from Napa Valley and Australia)

Dry and delicate
Most rosés from Provence

DESSERT WINES

Honey, caramel
Sauternes, ice wine, late harvest Riesling,
Chardonnay

Chocolate
Tawny Port, Madeira

Big, fruity, POW!
Port, late harvest Zinfandel

CHAPTER 4

Learning the Lingo

Taste is often a subjective experience. Depending on one's background and interests, your preference might be a Ford pickup truck over a Rolls Royce—it's not out of the question! However, with wines, true quality, regardless of taste, is measured by certain objective standards. This is not to say that simple table wines cannot please—in fact, they are manufactured for a broad appeal—but rather that fine wines please in ways that inexpensive wines rarely do.

Winetasting Techniques from the Pros

The five most common categories by which to judge a wine are complexity, concentration, length of finish, balance and harmony, and typicity. *Complexity* refers to the ways in which the wine changes in your glass over time. Inexpensive table wines are meant to be quaffable and simple, but the goal of a maker of fine wines is to create wines that have many layers that keep you curious and coming back sip after sip. Great wines have the power to leave you hypothesizing far beyond the last drop.

The *concentration* of a wine both improves its intensity and demonstrates the care of the winemaker for the quality of his or her product. Such wines come from vineyards where the cultivator has limited the yields of the vines. Planting vines close together forces the vines to compete with one another. The more stressed a vine is by the proximity of other vines, the more energy it focuses on its own production—concentrating its grapes with flavor and intensity. Grapes that have been nurtured (or stressed) in this way tend to produce wines with dense, concentrated flavors.

The *finish*, the amount of time that the taste of the wine lingers in your senses, can hint at the quality of the wine. The best wines keep expressing themselves long after leaving the mouth. In addition, the taste expressed ought to be *balanced*. The aim is for the alcoholic strength, acidity, residual sugar, and tannins to complement one another in such a way that no single element dominates all others in the wine.

Finally, *typicity*—the extent to which the wine displays characteristics typical to its region of origin, grape variety, and vintage (in a word, *terroir*)—indicates the greatness of a wine. Great wines are expressions of their soils, environments, climates, and the grapes and people that made them.

Thirsty for Knowledge?

There is a saying in the wine industry that Americans drink their white wine too cold and their red wine too hot. The best way to ensure that your whites and reds will be available at the perfect temperature when you're ready for them is to store the white and red wines separately, either in your wine cellar or in a wine fridge with two separate temperature control panels. Whites can be kept anywhere from 40–60° Fahrenheit; the key is that the temperature is consistent. But for real perfectionists, the conventional wisdom is that white wines are kept at 52–55° Fahrenheit, while reds are kept between 55–57° Fahrenheit.

Recognizing Flaws

Professional sommeliers often use words such as "like a barnyard," "dirt," and "tobacco," among others, to praise wines that most of us would consider offensive. With praise like that, how can you tell the difference between a strong wine that you don't like and one that has gone bad?

Problems That Are Fixable

There are certain distinctive smells that can give you a clue. The smell of asparagus denotes overripe grapes or wine kept too long in the bottle. A smell of burning matches or sulfur is caused by excesses of sulfur dioxide. Luckily, either decanting or swirling the glass might remove the odor. Hard-boiled or rotten egg-like odors are caused when sulfur attaches to hydrogen, creating hydrogen sulphide. If you have the patience, you could place a brass or copper object in the wine, and the odor should precipitate out as a fine sediment. Tartrates are harmless crystalline deposits that form during fermentation or aging. These crystals are made up of tartaric acids that are less soluble in wine than in water or juice. Many wineries remove these compounds with a process called cold stabilization. Straining the wine is the easiest way to remove these harmless crystals. Another harmless deposit is sediment, nonsoluble deposits consisting of crystalline and phenolic compounds that precipitate from the bottled wine over time. This is harmless and normal and can be fixed through decanting or straining. Unless occurring in a sparkling wine, refermentation or bubbles indicate that unspent yeast has not been removed, since it reacts with residual sugar and ferments for a second time, trapping gasses in the bottle. If the problem is minimal, use a Vacu Vin to remove the gas.

And Fix It Fast!

The smell of banana is caused by malolactic fermentation. While it can be pleasant when subtle, it tastes odd in larger amounts, particularly in red wines, and will often lead to a nail polish aroma. Although it's not a fault, it's not a good thing either—make Sangria promptly! A wine that tastes watery or weak implies that the winemaker allowed the yields from his or her vineyards to grow unacceptably high, or that it rained just before or during the harvest so that the grapes were diluted with rainwater. It's best to drink it as quickly as possible or use it for cooking.

Problems That Are Hopeless

The smell of Band-Aids, horse blanket, or manure (yes, this is distinctly different from an earthy or barnyardy Pinot Noir!) indicates the presence of brettanomyces, a wine-spoiling yeast. If the odor doesn't go away after several minutes, there isn't a cure. If you smell dirty socks, put the wine away; although there are a few causes (unclean barrels or bacterial contamination), you don't want to be ingesting any of them. Margarine-like smells are the result of excessive amounts of diacetyl, the buttery compound formed during the primary fermentation. Moldy odors are caused by bacterial spoilage, moldy grapes, or unclean barrels, while musty odors are caused by unclean barrels or cork in the wine. Nail polish odors are produced by intensive carbonic maceration, found in the worst Beaujolais Nouveau—don't go there! Onion, garlic, or burnt rubber smells are a serious fault caused by the reaction of alcohol to hydrogen sulphide (another wine fault) and create a foul-smelling compound called ethylmercaptain. If you smell rubbing alcohol, the alcohol level is out of balance, so pour it down the drain. You wouldn't drink regular rubbing alcohol, would you?

Sauerkraut odor comes from the lactic smell of excessive malolactic fermentation. Excessive acetaldehyde produces Sherry-like aromas, turning wines into vinegar. Sherry itself is protected from acetaldehyde by high alcohol levels, which prevent spoilage. A skunky smell is a sign of mercaptain compounds, terrible-smelling sulfur compounds that are created when hydrogen sulphide and other basic sulfur compounds combine to create an even worse problem. Vinegar is a sign of acetic acid bacteria, formed when fermentation is not handled correctly, the combination of alcohol, oxygen, and acetic acid bacteria.

Wet dog, or a musty or moldy odor and taste, can be a sign that the wine is corked. This is a common, naturally occurring wine fault. A corked wine is either oxidized—meaning it's stale because too much oxygen has already steeped into the wine via a faulty cork—or is exposed to chlorine-soaked corks in warm, moist conditions, allowing the formation of a chemical called 2-4-6 Trichloroanisole, or TCA. Corked wine is not to be confused with the phenomenon of "floating cork," which usually occurs due to improper opening technique, a harmless problem that is easily solved by removing the cork from your glass.

A filmy or oily slick on the surface of the wine is the result of improperly washed glasses. Rerinse the glass thoroughly in steaming hot water and use glass-drying cloths for those particular glasses. Although maderization is certainly acceptable in Madeira and vins doux naturels, in most wines oxidation is considered a fault: It occurs when wine is allowed to become exposed to warm temperatures, and acquires a cooked toffeelike flavor with some browning of the wine.

Naming Wines: Region Versus Grape, Old World Versus New World

Despite its international production, individual countries have yet to set a universal standard for designating wines. This can be confusing when faced with a wall of wine bottles in a store, but with a little background on the major countries you should be able to make an informed decision. The main thing to remember is that Old World wines (those from Europe) are mainly named according to their place of origin. New World wines (from Australia, Africa, and the Americas) are referred to by their grape variety.

Thirsty for Knowledge?

Did you know that Bordeaux are always made from five different grape varieties: Cabernet Sauvignon, Merlot, Cabernet Franc, Malbec, and Petit Verdot? Did you know that red Burgundy is always made from Pinot Noir? Did you know that Côtes du Rhône reds are always made from Syrah, Grenache, and Mouvedre? Did you know that although the same strict regulations do not occur in the states, the winemaking regions in the United States are also often divided by grape variety?

The reason for the difference is that Old World wine-makers have grown specific varieties in specific regions for generations. Adhering strictly to tradition ensures the best quality product from that soil. In the New World, experimentation reigns, and the regions are not yet established enough to indicate the production of a particular style or grape.

Of course, the more you know, the better you will be able to pick wines that you will enjoy. With that in mind, consider the following systems and how they are labeled.

Old World: Understanding the French System

Most French wines are labeled by their source rather than their grape variety. After all, France is known for its world-famous regions, not its grapes, although they too are used worldwide. Many people find French wine labels confusing (they are in French, after all!), but they are actually quite clear and simple once you know what you're looking for. See a French wine label decoded in Figure 4-1.

Fig. 4-1. *How to read a French wine label.*

Each French AOC—or Appellation d'Origine Contrôlée—wine label lists information on the producer, location, vintage, vineyard, and alcohol. All of these label features are required by law today, but that wasn't always true. In the late 1800s a series of viticultural maladies plagued Europe, devastating vineyards everywhere. The worst of these vine diseases was caused by the phylloxera louse, which destroyed nearly all of the vinifera vines in Europe. Meanwhile, because wine was in such short supply, demand increased, prices rose, and many French estates began making wine using grapes from other regions and bottling them as their own.

To combat fraud and guarantee product authenticity, the French government intervened in 1905 and laid out the framework for the current AOC system. In 1935, an organization called the Institut National des Appellations d'Origin (INAO) was created to define regional boundaries based on terroir. They were also responsible for restricting maximum yields and alcohol levels, and they have defined appropriate grape varieties and viticultural, vinification, and maturation practices.

In addition to the AOC, there are three lesser categories of wine law in France. Vin Délimité de Qualité Supérieure, or VDQS, is a steppingstone to AOC. The VDQS laws cover the same things as AOC but are less stringent. Below that are Vin de Pays, or country wines. Under this labeling, producers have much more control over the grapes they can use and can even place the grape variety on the label.

Below Vin de Pays is the basic Vin de Table. These table wines are rarely exported and are loosely controlled. Because of the large amount of high-quality, affordable AOC wine being produced today, the Vin de Table is in decline.

The Bottom Line

French wine labels display the vintage, appellation, producer, and alcohol level. Some French wines have specific names, and all state that they originated in France.

In addition, the quality level will appear. The quality level is administered to the wine by the French AOC, which judges wines based on the terroir where the grapes were harvested. French quality levels also vary by region. Distinctive quality levels include Premier Cru, Grand Cru, Cru Classé, Cru Bourgeois, Premier Grand Cru Classé, Premier Grand Cru, Cru Artisan, and Grand Cru Classé. However, the quality of a specific region's table wine might be sufficient for your purposes—that's where the region guide in Part 2 will come in handy!

Champagne Labels—a Little Bit Different

Champagne labels vary from those produced for other regions.

Fig. 4-2. *How to read a Champagne label.*

They carry two added designations: color and sugar level. The color also explains which grapes were used. Categories include Blanc de Blanc (100 percent Chardonnay), Blanc de Noir (100 percent Pinot Noir), and Rosé. The sugar levels, from low to high are brut nature, extra brut, brut, sec (dry), demi-sec (rich), extra sec (extra dry), doux, and non-dosage.

Old World: Understanding Italian Wine

The appellations of Italy are somewhat disorganized and quite confusing. It is often hard to tell whether the name on an Italian wine is its region or grape variety. Frequently it is both! Italy has so many regions, wines, and styles that it would take a lifetime to know them all, but what better joy for a wine lover than to try!

Fig. 4-3. *Decoding an Italian wine label.*

Like France, Italy has a controlled appellation system with several levels of quality. Quality wines from defined regions are listed as Denominazione di Origine Controllata (DOC). A step above that is Denominazione di Origine Controllata e Garantita (DOCG), which follows stricter rules than DOC regions. There are now just over twenty DOCGs and the number is growing.

Vino da Tavola generally indicates ordinary table wine made outside the regulations of a DOC appellation, although some great wine producers were forced to use the Vino da Tavola label because they used methods or grape varieties that are forbidden within a particular DOC region. The term *Super Tuscan* was coined when several producers did just that within the region of Tuscany. These winemakers wanted to use grapes that were not allowed in the region and decided to take the lower status instead of sacrificing the quality of the wines. Because of that, another quality level, Indicazione Geografica Tipica (IGT), was created for wines like the Super Tuscans that are produced with higher-quality standards than Vino da Tavola yet do not meet all the regulations of the DOC and DOCG appellations.

There are also several common terms that appear on Italian wine labels. *Riserva* is a word describing a wine that has been aged for longer periods of time. *Classico* refers to a geographic region in which the proportion of fine wines is higher than elsewhere. *Superiore* is also often seen on labels and usually refers to a higher alcohol content, and sometimes to extra aging. Sparkling wines usually come in one of two forms: the lightly sparkling and fizzy Frizzante and the fully sparkling Spumante.

The Bottom Line

Italian wine quality is, from low to high, designated by the terms Classico, Riserva, Riserva Speciale, and Superiore. Italian sparkling wine differentiates between bubble levels (frizzantino, frizzante, and spumante) and sugar levels (amaro, ascuitto, secco, abboccato, auslese, pastoso, semi-socco, and dolce).

Old World: Understanding Spanish Wine

In a sincere effort to control and monitor its wine production, Spain introduced the Denominación de Origen system in 1926. This series of laws is roughly the same as France's appellations d'origines system, which allocates specific types of wine to specific regions, and ranks the wineries within them on a quality-based scale.

Spain's vineyards are mostly classified according to a four-level system. Vino de Mesa is the base level and can be compared to France's Vin de Table. Within this designation is a second level in which winemakers residing within a Denominación de Origen (DO) region may produce whatever type of wine they want, regardless of the specific requirements of the DO. Vino Comarcal is the second official level of wine production and is equivalent to Vin de Pays in France. Next is Vino de la Tierra, and finally, the top wines receive the Denominación de Origen designation. Denominación de Origen Calificada (DOCa) is the very best rating, and so far only Rioja and Priorat have reached this level.

Fig. 4-4. *Decoding a Spanish wine label.*

Certain terms that appear on the labels denote specific characteristics of the wine, making it easier to understand what's in the bottle. *Vino de Cosecha* ensures that at least 85 percent of the grapes used have been harvested in the year on the label. These are generally young wines. *Crianza* means that the wine was released after at least six months in oak barrels and two years in a bottle, although some regions have increased the aging requirement. A wine with *Reserva* on the label means that it is a red wine aged for minimum of three years, and *Gran Reserva* wines, which are only designated in exemplary years, are aged for three years in barrels and two years in bottles.

As displayed by the Cava label, Spanish sparkling wines include the quality distinctions Vino Joven, Crianza, Reserva, and Gran Reserva, in addition to the sweetness levels brut, secco, semi-secco, semiduke, and dulce.

Old World: Understanding Portuguese Wine

Portugal's wine laws today are based on the French Appellation d'Origin Contrôlée.

Fig. 4-5. *Decoding a Portuguese table wine label.*

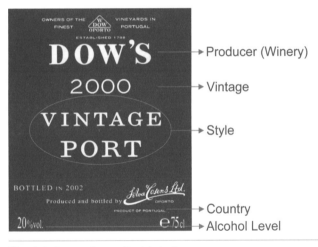

Fig. 4-6. *Decoding a Port label.*

The quality of Portuguese table wines includes Vinho de Mesa, Garrafeira, Reserva, and Velho. Port, however, is differentiated by style rather than quality, although quality is inherent in the style, as we saw in Chapter 2. Possible styles are Ruby, Tawny, Vintage, Vintage Character, Late-Bottled Vintage (LBV), Crusted, Single-Quinta, Single-Quinta Tawny, and White.

Portugal's Denominação de Origem Controlada (DOC) determines regional boundaries, the varieties allowed to be grown, the permissible viticultural practices, the appropriate range of alcohol level, and the information that the label must contain.

The three basic categories of Portuguese wine are Vinho de Mesa, Vinho Regional, and Denominação de Origem Controlada. The lowest level is Vinho de Mesa (table wine). For these wines, grapes can come from anywhere in Portugal and the winery need not even include a vintage. Next is Vinho Regional (regional wine), in which 85 percent of grapes must come from the region specified on the label. Regional wines, however, are not subject to the strict requirements of a Denominação de Origem Controlada wine, in which all the grapes must come entirely from the region on the label.

The wine regions of Portugal are determined by the clear climatic divisions. In the northern part of the country, the climate is maritime with warm summers and cool, wet winters. In some areas rainfall can reach 100 inches a year. Toward the south it's a different story, as rainfall is lower and summer temperatures are much higher. For hundreds of years, Portugal has enjoyed international fame for its Port wines and its fortified Madeira; today, its red table wines are rapidly gaining in popularity.

Old World: Understanding German Wine

German wine labels are notoriously difficult to make sense of, but once you get the hang of it they actually reveal as much as or more about the wine than the labels of any other country. As in Spain, the wines are separated into categories regarding quality.

German wine labels will, like most, include the producer (or winery), the vintage, the varietal, the region (or appellation), and the alcohol level. In addition, the label contains quality level, sugar level, and, for sparkling wines, sekt (sweetness) levels. The possible quality designations, from low to high, are Deutscher Tafelwein, Landwein, Qualitätswein bestimmter Anbaugebiete (QbA), and Prädikatswein (renamed in 2007 from Qualitätswein mit Prädikat, or QmP). The sugar levels, from dry to sweet, are Kabinett, Auslese, Spätlese, Beerenauslese, Eiswein, and Trockenbeerenauslese. For sparkling wines, the categories, again from dry to sweet, are extra brut, extra herb, brut, herb, extra trocken (dry), trocken (dry), halbtrocken (demi-sec), süss, drux, and doux (sweet).

Fig. 4-7. *Decoding a German wine label.*

At the highest level of quality is the Prädikatswein designation. In addition to the region and vineyard, a German wine label at this level also includes an extra category called Prädikat, indicating the ripeness of the grapes at the time they were picked. Generally, the riper the grapes, the sweeter the wine. In order of increasing sugar concentration, the Prädikat categories are Kabinett, Spätlase, Auslese, Beerenauslese, Eiswein, and Trockenbeerenauslese.

At one extreme, the Kabinett is nearly bone dry. At the other end, Trockenbeerenauslese, or "selected dried berries," are picked late in the season after they become fully infected with noble rot. In these cases, the skin has cracked and the water has partially evaporated, leaving behind more concentrated grapes. Wine from these berries is golden and honeyed, high in alcohol, and lusciously sweet. In some years a frost or rot kills off the late crop and no Trockenbeerenauslese can be made—the high price in other years compensates winemakers for the risk of leaving fruit on the vine so late into the autumn.

What's the Charta System?

In addition to the Prädikat system, Germany has now implemented the Charta system. In order for a wine to be classified as a Charta wine, several conditions must be met. The wine must be dry and of a sweetness that would normally lead to a classification of Kabinett or Spätlase. The grapes must be entirely from the bottling estate, and they all must be Riesling. There are also residual sugar and acidity levels that must be maintained. What all this comes down to is that any wine labeled "Charta" will be an excellent dry Riesling. If you see the Charta signature double arch on a white label, you know you're in for a memorable wine experience.

Old World: Understanding Austrian Wine

Although the Austrian system follows that of Germany, the main difference is that Kabinett is a part of the Qualitätswein category. A new system was initiated in 2003, the Districtus Austria Controllatus (DAC), which considers terroir as opposed to ripeness levels.

New World: Understanding American Wine

Although wine has been made in California since the late nineteenth century, until 1980 there was no American version of the French appellation system. A wine could be labeled "California" if the grapes were entirely grown in the state, or it could be labeled "Napa County" if three-quarters of the grapes were grown in Napa County. Vineyards do not always follow political borders, however, and wines made from grapes that were half grown in Sonoma and half grown in Napa had a very tough time indeed. They could call themselves California wines, but this would be selling them short—they didn't want to have to hide the fact that they came from two of the top regions in the state.

In 1978, the Bureau of Alcohol, Tobacco and Firearms authorized the creation of American Viticultural Areas (AVAs), the rough equivalent of a French appellation. These AVAs can be large or small, and they can overlap.

For instance, most of Napa County is included in the Napa Valley AVA. Inside that large region there are many smaller AVAs. A wine from Rutherford, for example, comes from the Rutherford AVA inside the Napa AVA and can be labeled as either. An extreme case is the Carneros AVA, which overlaps with the AVAs of Napa Valley, Sonoma, Sonoma Coast, and the North Coast. In any case, if the grapes are grown and bottled on the same winemaker's property in a single AVA, the wine may be labeled "Estate Bottled."

The AVA system is far less authoritarian than the French AOC—the bureau largely refrains from dictating specific practices to follow, such as which varietals can be planted. For this reason, an AVA is not necessarily a good predictor of taste or variety, and a large AVA may contain many varieties and microclimates.

As a consumer, the AVA can be a useful tool. If a wine is marked "Rutherford," you know that 85 percent of its grapes are produced within that region. If the AVA is large, like the California North/Central Coast AVA, the name won't necessarily tell you much about the wine. From a winemaker's perspective, the decision of which AVA to list is an important one. A prestigious area like Rutherford, for example, benefited from lobbying for its own AVA, which helped for branding purposes. For a lesser-known area in Napa, the distinction may be less overt.

New World: Understanding the Rest of the New World

New World wines are far simpler to decode than Old World wines. The United States requires a brand name (for example, Iron Horse Vineyards), a designation (red table wine), alcohol content (exact percentage by volume), and amount of foreign as opposed to American grapes in cases where the two are blended. The vintage year is given if 95 percent of the grapes (or more) were harvested in that year. Most producers choose to include the variety (or varieties) of grapes used as well. Other New World wine labels (though the phrasing might change) tend to include the same information, particularly if they are being sold in the United States.

The rest of the New World wine-producing countries follow the example set by America. Labeled by the grape from which they come, the region still appears on the label, and for good reason: The difference between New Zealand's Hawke's Bay and Marlborough Sauvignon Blancs, for example, can be quite dramatic.

Wine Label Wrap-Up

Whether you walk into a wine shop, supermarket, or restaurant (or even look at a Web site!), the multitude of wines can be overwhelming. Sometimes stores will write a review or have a rating for specific wines, but that information is rarely available for each bottle. So how best to make sense of them all? Many people pick their wine by the label, but there's a difference between appreciating the picture on the label and making an informed decision about the wine from the label. Luckily, in recognition of that fact, each country requires specific information to be shown on the bottle. This helps the winemaker advertise the contents of the bottle and helps the consumer to make a more informed decision. The bottom line is that there is no shame in choosing an unknown wine by its label—you should be! In addition to how aesthetically pleasing the label is, hopefully now you will be empowered to also decode the label depending upon its region of origin. This type of label judging will ideally lead you into the land of a truly tasty bottle of wine.

CHAPTER 5

Red Grape Varieties Revealed

All wine grapes have signature characteristics that they impart to a wine: body, flavor, texture—and, in the case of red wine grapes, color and tannins. You can predict how a wine is likely to taste by the grapes that are crushed to make it. You'll find a grape's true character in a wine regardless of winemaking practices. You may not always see the grape name on the label, but each variety contributes something special to the mix.

Cabernet Sauvignon

For a wine that has consistently captivated audiences around the world, you'd expect Cabernet Sauvignon (Cab for short) to have a long history. Not so. It's less than six hundred years old, which in wine terms makes it relatively young.

One Tough Customer

The Cabernet grapes are small, black, and very tough-skinned. The thick skins make Cab grapes pretty resistant to disease and capable of withstanding hard autumn rains, which is a good thing because the grapes don't ripen until long into the growing season. The skins are also what give the wine its highly tannic nature. Cab grapes are adaptable, growing in almost any climate that's not too cool. They grow in most major wine-producing regions of the world. Even in Spain and Italy where local grapes have dominated the landscape for centuries, Cabernet is now being planted and used in nontraditional blends.

The planting of Cabernet Sauvignon got a real jump-start in the 1800s when it was used to replant the vineyards of Europe that had been ravaged by phylloxera. It became the primary grape of the famous Bordeaux blends from Médoc and Graves. Today, its popularity has spread around the world—particularly to the Napa Valley, California, where high-quality (and sometimes super-high priced) Cabs reign.

The Wines

Because of their high tannins, Cabernets start out life fairly harshly. Aging—first in oak barrels and later in bottles—softens and smoothes them. Serious Cabs can age for fifteen years or more. Think of Rod Stewart as a Cab. In his youth, he was an in-your-face rocker. In his maturity, he's crooning mellow ballads. Same voice, same showman, but age has added subtlety.

Typical tasting comments on young Cabernets usually praise the black currant, bell pepper, chocolate, and spice flavors. Older vintages are often described as having a taste of tobacco.

While 100 percent Cabernet wines are made (many in California), current trends lean toward blending. Bordeaux has always blended its Cabernet wine with Merlot, Cabernet Franc, Petit Verdot, or Malbec. Merlot often softens the Cabernet's fruit character; Cabernet Franc adds wonderful aromatics (often vegetal, but good vegetal as opposed to flawed vegetal); Malbec offers inky color and tannin; Petit Verdot adds serious backbone, enhancing longevity.

Thirsty for Knowledge?

Petit Verdot derives its name from the size of the berries, which are small (hence the "petit") and highly concentrated. Petit Verdot is also characterized by thick skins and a serious pow in fruit character. For this reason, it often serves as the backbone in Bordeaux and Bordeaux-style wines. Aside from the berry size, there is nothing "petit" about Petit Verdot!

In Australia, Shiraz is added to the Cabernet, giving the wine a spicy pepper flavor. In Italy, winemakers have introduced Cabernet to their Sangiovese-based wines, producing a new breed of wine referred to as Super Tuscans. In Spain, Cabernet is blended with the native Tempranillo.

A SAMPLING OF CABERNETS

Fisher Vineyards Coach Insignia Cabernet Sauvignon (Napa Valley)—$70.00

Corison Cabernet Sauvignon (Napa Valley)—$70.00

Highbank Vineyards Cabernet Sauvignon (Coonawarra, Australia)—$50

Pretty Sally Cabernet Sauvignon (Central Victoria, Australia)—$23.00

Las Perdices Cabernet Sauvignon (Mendoza, Argentina)—$18.50

Merlot

The 1990s thrust Merlot into the spotlight as it became the easy-drinking red variety of choice, a less tannic alternative to Cabernet. Its mass-market appeal led to vastly increased planting around the world. In California alone, Merlot acreage rose from 2,000 acres in 1985 to 50,000 in 2003.

Second Fiddle No More

Merlot's small, dark-blue grapes are relatively thin-skinned, making them earlier ripening and less tannic than Cabernet Sauvignon. Merlot can be traced back to first-century France, but it wasn't named as a distinct variety until the 1800s.

While Cabernet gained recognition in Bordeaux's Médoc district, Merlot became prominent in the cooler Bordeaux districts of Pomerol and Saint-Émilion, and it is the third most planted red grape in France. In addition to France, Merlot is important in California, Washington, New York's Long Island, northeastern Italy, and Chile.

Merlot has a reputation for low acidity and softness. It makes beautiful wines all by itself or blended with others—sort of the Miss Congeniality of the wine world. With its soaring popularity, however, came overproduction in some areas and a tarnished image for many undistinguished wines that were shaped more by market forces than the winemaker's art.

Typical descriptions of Merlot flavors are plum, black cherry, currant, violet, and rose.

MERLOTS WITH DISTINCTION

Blackbird Merlot (Napa Valley, California)—$80.00

Schug Merlot (Sonoma County, California)—$25.00

Seven Sisters Merlot (South Africa)—$17.99

Pinot Noir

Pinot Noir has been frustrating winemakers since the ancient Romans cultivated it. Pinot is recognized world-wide as a premier, yet finicky, grape. Pinot presents obstacles to winemaking every step of the way—from its propagation to bottle aging.

Pinot Noir first earned its reputation for making magnificent wines in the Burgundy region of France and, more specifically, the two-mile-wide stretch called the Côte d'Or. Pinot Noir is also grown in the Champagne region, where it's one of the three grape varieties allowed to be used in its sparkling wine.

A Handful of Trouble

How difficult can Pinot Noir be? Let's count some of the ways. It's finicky about where it's planted and requires a long, cool growing season. The vine is genetically unstable, making the fruit from parent and offspring vines inconsistent. It's susceptible to bugs, spring frost, and disease. It lacks sufficient leaf cover to protect the grapes from birds. Even if the fruit survives the birds, the thin-skinned grapes can shrivel and dry out.

Thus Pinot Noir produces the best wines when it's grown in limestone soil and in relatively cool climates. Outside of France it's grown in such areas as Germany, Austria, Italy, eastern Europe, South America, South Africa, Australia, Canada, and the United States. Its emergence in America began in the 1930s in California, and it has gained prominence farther north in the Willamette Valley of Oregon.

You might wonder, with all its difficulties, why anyone would go to all the trouble of producing a wine from Pinot Noir. One sip will give you the answer. Pinot Noir is like a demanding diva. She may be a complete pain in the neck prior to her performance, but it's all worth it as soon as she sings her first note.

Pinot Noir has been described as liquid silk. The texture is soft and velvety. Because the grape is less pigmented than other red wine grapes, the wine is lighter in color too. Pinot is full-bodied but not heavy. It can be high in alcohol, yet neither acidic nor tannic. Typical Pinot Noir flavors are raspberries, Bing cherries, and smoke.

PICKING THE PERFECT PINOT

Dry River Pinot Noir (Martinborough, New Zealand)—$85

Spring Mountain Estate Bottled Pinot Noir (Napa Valley, California)—$60

Inspiration Vineyards Pinot Noir (Carneros, California)—$25.00

Louis Jadot Beaujolais Villages Moulin-a-Vent 2004 (Beaune, France)—$17.99

Syrah/Shiraz

It's called Shiraz in Australia, but everywhere else in the world the grape is known as Syrah. It has been present in France's Rhône Valley since at least Roman times. The grape arrived in Australia in the 1800s and became one of the most widely planted varieties in the country. Not too long after that, Syrah arrived in the United States. In the last five years, American-produced Syrah has become very fashionable.

Syrah has all sorts of legends attached to it. One legend has it that Syrah was brought by the Crusaders from Shiraz, Persia, to the Rhône. Another says the ancient Romans brought it from Syracuse in Sicily. DNA testing has shown that Syrah is really a native of the Rhône Valley.

Survivor

The Syrah grape is black, thick-skinned, and can survive almost anywhere. That's why you'll find Syrah in places as diverse as France, Australia, and northern and southern California. Even within those areas, Syrah thrives both in cool climates and in warm and sunny conditions.

In the northern Rhône, Syrah is rarely blended, and it is used in the wines from Cornas, Côte-Rôtie, Hermitage, and Crozes-Hermitage. When young, the wines are deeply colored and tannic with a distinct spiciness. As they age, they ease into flavors of blackberries, plums, and smoke. In the southern Rhône, Syrah is blended with other varietals to produce such well-known wines as Châteauneuf-du-Pape. In Australia, Shiraz is made in two distinct styles: the big, rich, tannic style and the lighter, fruitier, drink-me-now style.

QUE SERA, SYRAH

Zacherle Syrah (Sonoma County, California)—$40.00

Kingston Family Vineyards Bayo Oscuro Syrah (Casablanca, Chile)—$32.00

Pretty Sally Shiraz (Central Victoria, Australia)—$24.50

Six Master Shiraz (Hunter Valley, Australia)—$21.00

Thorny Devil Shiraz (Western Australia, Australia)—$13.99

Watershed NVD Shades Cabernet Merlot Shiraz (Margaret River, Australia)—$13.00

Sangiovese

Sangiovese is one of Italy's oldest red varieties and is said to have been cultivated by the Etruscans, the early inhabitants of the Italian peninsula. It wasn't until about 1600 that Sangiovese finally got its name. It comes from the Latin *sanguis Jovis*—"blood of Jupiter." Sangiovese grows all over its native Italy, but its real home base is in Tuscany. Only recently has the grape's popularity risen dramatically in the United States.

All in the Family

Sangiovese is the main component of Chianti. Sangiovese has a lot of subvarieties. Both Vino Nobile de Montepulciano and the potent and long-lived Brunello di Montalcino are made with it. For the most part, wines made with Sangiovese have pronounced tannins and acidity but not great depth of color. In the 1960s, Italian winemakers began producing 100 percent Sangiovese wines and also blending the grape with Cabernet Sauvignon—wines that became known as Super Tuscans.

SAMPLING SANGIOVESE

Pazzo by Bacio Divino (Napa Valley) (Sangiovese/ Cabernet Sauvignon/Zinfandel/Petit Sirah/Viognier) —$34.00

Le Fonti Chianti Classico (Tuscany, Italy)—$30.00

Borgo Reale Chianti Classico (Tuscany, Italy)—$22.00

Banfi Chianti Classico (Tuscany, Italy)—$18.00

Colle Pino, Sangiovese/Merlot 2005 (Chianti, Italy)—$9.00

Tempranillo

Tempranillo has been called Spain's answer to Cabernet Sauvignon. It's the country's most important red grape variety and is the main grape in Rioja wines. It was once rarely used outside of Spain except for blending. Today it's making itself known in California, Australia, and South America.

The Name Game

Tempranillo (from the Spanish word *temprano*) means "early"—so named because it ripens earlier than most red varieties. Tempranillo has a bewildering array of aliases. Inside Spain it goes by Cencibel, Ojo de Liebre ("eye of the hare"), Tinta de Pais, Tinto Fino, Tinta de Toro, and Tinto de Madred. In Portugal it's known as Tinta Roriz. It's also been grown in California for grape juice and jug wines and called Valdepeñas.

TEMPRANILLO WINES TO TRY

Luis Alegre Tempranillo Selected Vintage Rioja (Spain)—$42.00

Almagre Red Wine Crianza Tempranillo DOC Rioja 2001 (Spain)—$20

Zinfandel

Zinfandel is the all-American grape—well, sort of. Although Zinfandel was brought to California from elsewhere in the 1800s, the BATF (Bureau of Alcohol, Tobacco and Firearms, which administers wine-labeling regulations) classified Zinfandel as a native grape. After its introduction to America, it became a huge success. It was easy to grow, produced big crops, and could be made into an amazing number of different styles.

However, Prohibition, the Depression, and World War II put an end to all that. Zinfandel vineyards might have disappeared if it hadn't been for an unexpected marketing phenomenon in the 1970s, White Zinfandel, which sparked a new interest in Zinfandel (both colors).

Zin's True Identity Is Revealed

Southern Italy produces a dry red wine from the Primitivo grape that was thought to be related to Zinfandel. Cousins? Brothers? Nope. The same grape. DNA investigation revealed them to be identical. Their ancestor was discovered later: a wild vine that grows on the Adriatic Coast in Croatia in the former Yugoslavia.

Zinfandel is a chameleon. It can be vinified in many styles, from a light, claret-style wine to a high-alcohol monster. The more robust styles have berry and spicy black pepper flavors.

ZINFANDEL VERSUS PRIMITIVO

Storybook Mountain Vineyards Estate Reserve Zinfandel (Napa Valley, California)—$45.00

Battaglini Estate Winery Proprietor Reserve Zinfandel (Russian River Valley, California)—$40.00

Inspiration Vineyards Zinfandel (Alexander Valley, California)—$24.00

St. Barthelemy Zinfandel Port (California)—$20.00

Other Red Grape Varieties

Each variety of vinifera has its own characteristics and something unique to bring to a wine. More often than not, wines are blended so that the final product—the sum of all the parts—is greater than any single wine by itself. Perhaps a wine's contribution is acid, texture, or tannins. Here are some other red grape varieties that put their distinctive mark on wines.

Barbera

Barbera is an Italian grape that contributes deep garnet colors, a medium to full body, and light tannin levels. In warmer growing areas, it develops high sugar levels and, consequently, high alcohol levels. Barbera makes Italy's Barbera d'Asti, Barbera d'Alba, and Barbera del Monferrato.

Cascin Adelaide Barbera d'Alba 2002 (Italy)—$25.00

Carignan

Originally from northern Spain, this high-yielding vine grows extensively in France and around the Mediterranean. It's popular as a blending grape because it brings red fruit characteristics, deep purple color, strong tannin structure, and high levels of alcohol. Carignan is also known as Carignane, Carignano, Carinena, Mazuelo, and Monestel.

Carmenère

A historic variety once heavily planted in Bordeaux, Carmenère was one of the six varieties allowed for use in making red Bordeaux wines. Because of low yields and ripening problems, it was almost completely abandoned in Bordeaux, but it has found a new home in Chile. Imported in 1850, it was mislabeled as Merlot until 1991. Carmenère produces deeply colored, full-bodied wines.

Gamay

Gamay is the French variety solely responsible for the distinctive wines of Beaujolais, which are light- to medium-bodied, high in acid, low in tannins, and meant to be drunk young. Beaujolais Nouveau is a special category of new Gamay wine (seven to nine weeks old) that is released on the third Thursday of each November.

Grenache

Grenache is a sweet grape that can produce wines with 15 or 16 percent alcohol because of its high sugar level. It's one of the official blending partners in Châteauneuf du-Pape. In Spain it's known as Garnacha, where it's blended with Tempranillo to produce the red Rioja wines.

Malbec

A French grape permitted as one of the blending grapes in the famous wines of Bordeaux, Malbec is soft yet robust, intense, and full-bodied. Malbec has found a new home in Argentina where it is extensively produced as a rich and earthy varietal.

MOUTHWATERING MALBECS

Enrique Foster Malbec (Mendoza, Argentina)—$50.00

Sur de Los Andes Gran Reserva Malbec (Mendoza, Argentina)—$22.99

Paul Hobbs El Felino Malbec (Mendoza, Argentina)—$17.00

Nebbiolo

A thick-skinned grape grown mainly in Italy's Piedmont region, Nebbiolo is used as a varietal and for blending with other Italian wines. It is most famous for making two of Italy's great reds: Barolo and Barbaresco. It generally needs long aging in wood to soften.

NOT-TO-BE-MISSED NEBBIOLO

Cascina Adelaide Langhe Nebbiolo (Italy)—$24.00

Pinotage

A uniquely South African grape created in the 1920s by crossing Pinot Noir and Cinsault, Pinotage has a distinct spicy and peppery flavor. Although winemakers elsewhere have been experimenting with Pinotage, it remains primarily a product of South Africa.

Seven Sisters Pinotage (South Africa)—$14.99

CHAPTER 6

Getting to Know White Grape Varieties

Grapes are the dominant factor in determining a wine's taste. Different varieties have different aromas, flavors, and colors—the grape's varietal character. Even though varietal character is fairly predictable within limits, it's not precise. Every grape variety has multiple clones that will affect the taste. Grapes picked at various times throughout the harvest can influence taste, and so can a winemaker's techniques. With all of that taken into account, take a look at what you can expect from some prominent white varieties.

Chardonnay

DNA profiling has concluded that Chardonnay is a cross between a member of the Pinot family and an ancient, nearly extinct, variety called Gouais Blanc. Gouais Blanc originated in Croatia and was probably brought to France by the Romans. The first recorded reference to Chardonnay was in 1330. Some historical theories claim that Chardonnay even came from Lebanon.

The Chameleon

As they say in the wine business, Chardonnay is low in varietal character. That means that the grapes have fairly neutral flavors that are less identifiable than other grape varieties. A lot of what determines the taste of a Chardonnay is what the winemaker does to the grapes. Using oak to ferment or age the wine (or at both points!) produces a richness and the familiar oak flavors of toast and vanilla. Leaving the wine on the lees adds complexity; conducting malolactic fermentation reduces the overall acidity and produces a softer, creamier wine. All these are flavors not derived from the grapes themselves.

Location, Location, Location

Chardonnay is hardy, versatile, and can grow successfully in all but the most extreme wine regions around the world. It can make great—though different—wines almost anywhere within the range in which it is most comfortable. Cool-climate Chardonnays tend toward a dry crispness and clean fruit flavors, while warmer-climate Chardonnays lean toward richer honey and butterscotch flavors.

In Burgundy, where it's *the* noble white wine grape, Chardonnay is a part of all the region's great white wines, such as Montrachet, Meursault, Pouilly-Fuissé, and Chablis. It's one of the three grapes—along with Pinot Noir and Pinot Meunier—allowed in Champagne and the only grape in blanc de blanc.

ABC

You've probably heard the mantra "anything but Chardonnay." Chardonnay is thought of as ubiquitous, boring, and overoaked. Particularly compatible with oak, Chardonnay usually receives some oak treatment—with the exceptions of Chardonnay wines from northern Italy, Chablis, and France's Mâconnais district. Recently a bunch of unoaked Chardonnays have entered the arena and are gaining momentum.

Chardonnay didn't become the most popular white wine in the world for no reason. You can expect a tremendous variety of flavors, medium to high acidity, medium to full body, and minimal fruit to tropical fruit. And you can count on a wine that's dry.

QUINTESSENTIAL EXAMPLES OF
CALIFORNIA CHARDONNAYS

Fisher Vineyard "Whitney's Vineyard" Chardonnay
(Napa Valley, California)—$70.00

Château Potelle Winery "VGS" Chardonnay
(Napa Valley)—$35.00

Fantesca Estate Chardonnay (Napa Valley)—$35.00

Sullivan Private Reserve Chardonnay
(Napa Valley)—$30.00

SOME UNOAKED CHARDONNAYS

Te Awa Unoaked Chardonnay (Hawke's Bay, New
Zealand)—$24.00

Wayne Gretzky Estates Direct No. 99 Unoaked Chardonnay (Ontario, Canada)—$24.00

Gunn Estate Unoaked Chardonnay (Hawke's Bay,
New Zealand)—$18.00

Thirsty for Knowledge?

Oak barrels are a winemaker's spice rack. Just like a chef might prefer certain spices, winemakers often prefer to work with specific coopers of specific types of barrels. Barrels come in light, medium, and dark wood and are further flavored by their degree of chauf ("toast" in French): light, medium, or dark. Some really zealous winemakers even build relationships with the coopers such that they can choose the tree from which their barrels are made! Each French oak barrel costs approximately $1,200 today; American and Hungarian oak barrels are in the $400–$600 range. Many winemakers only keep barrels for two to three years. After a mere year, barrels often lose 80 percent of their economic value. Barrels are a really expensive investment in winemaking, needless to say!

Chenin Blanc

The traditional home of Chenin Blanc is the Loire Valley of France, where it's been cultivated among picturesque châteaux since the Middle Ages. Chenin Blanc is a sturdy grape with high natural acidity and the versatility to produce crisp, dry table wines, sparkling wines, and sweet dessert wines. In France you'll find dry Chenin Blancs from Saumur and Savennières, off-dry wines from Vouvray and Anjou, dessert wines from Coteaux du Layon, and sparkling wines labeled Crémant de Loire.

Outside of France, Chenin Blanc is often used as a blending grape with only a small percentage of it going into varietal bottlings. South Africa, however, produces a full range of Chenin Blanc wines, referring to the grape as Steen. It's even used in their fortified wines and spirits.

The Model of Cooperation

Chenin Blanc is a cooperative sort of grape. It ripens in the middle of the season so that no extraordinary harvesting measures have to be taken. With its compact clusters it's easy to pick. The grapes have tough skins that minimize damage as they make their way to the crusher, and their natural acidity helps the aging process. A number of California producers make the classic dry style of Chenin Blanc that typifies the Loire.

CHECK OUT SOME OF THESE CHARMING CHENINS

Chappellet Dry Chenin Blanc (Napa Valley)—$16.00

Ayama Chenin Blanc (Western Australia)—$15.00

Seven Sisters "Yolanda" Chenin Blanc (South Africa)—$12.00

Gewürztraminer

Most people either love Gewürztraminer . . . or hate it. It has an intense aroma and strong flavors and is fairly difficult to enjoy with food. Sommeliers typically suggest pairing Gewürztraminer with highly seasoned food and spicy Asian and Mexican dishes.

The grape is thought to be a mutated form of the Traminer grape. Due to its taste, *gewürz* (meaning "spicy") was attached to it by Alsatians in the nineteenth century. The name caught on, but it wasn't until 1973 that the term *Gewürztraminer* was officially adopted.

Sweet and Spicy

The first thing you'll notice is that Gewürztraminer smells like flowers. When you taste it, you'll see that it can be sweet and spicy at the same time. Not all Gewürztraminers are sweet. It depends on who's making them.

Alsace has had arguably the most success with Gewürztraminer. Producers there make it dry—unless they're using the grapes for dessert wines, in which case the wines are exceptionally sweet.

In Germany, Gewürztraminers are usually off-dry to medium sweet. They have less alcohol and more acidity than their Alsatian counterparts. The high acidity camouflages the perception of all that sweetness.

Because Gewürztraminer grows best in cool climates, it has found good homes in Austria, eastern Europe, New Zealand, Canada, and the United States—especially Oregon, Washington, and New York. A few U.S. producers offer a dry version of the wine, but most produce Gewürztraminer with a perceptible sweetness.

Muscat

Muscat is the world's oldest-known grape variety and has grown around the Mediterranean for centuries. Early records show Muscat was shipped from the port of Frontignan in southwest France during the time of Charlemagne. Actually, Muscat is a family of grapes with more than two hundred varieties. The grapes range from white to almost black. And the wines vary from fine and light— even sparkling—to deep, dark, and sweet. Muscat is the only variety that produces aromas and flavors in wine just like the grape itself. Among the most familiar of the Muscat varieties are the following:

Muscat Blanc à Petits Grains: Considered the best of the Muscats, it's responsible for the sweet, fortified Muscat de Beaumes-de-Venise, for Italy's sparkling Asti, and for Clairette de Die. The grape is also known as Muscat Blanc, Muscat Canelli, Moscat d'Alsace, and Moscatel Rosé, among others.

Muscat of Alexandria: Thought to date back to ancient Egypt, it's most widely grown in Spain and is one of the three varieties permitted in making Sherry.

The grape also goes by Moscatel de Málaga, Moscatel, Moscatel Romano, Moscatel Gordo, and Gordo Blanc, among others.

Muscat Ottonel: A lighter flavored grape, it is also called Muskotaly. Muscat Ottonel is used for dry, perfumey wines in Alsace and dessert wines in Austria.

Muscat Hamburg: Used primarily as table grapes, eastern European winemakers produce thin red wines from it. It's also called Black Muscat and Moscato di Amburgo.

BOTTLENOTES' FAVORITE MUSCAT

Feiler-Artinger NVD Muscat-Ottonel Spätlese (Austria)—$28.00

Pinot Gris

The French call it Pinot Gris. The Italians call it Pinot Grigio. Americans produce both and drink a lot of it. The Pinot Gris grape exhibits a range of colors from grayish blue to brownish pink. It's in the same family as Pinot Noir and Pinot Blanc but has a character all its own. Pinot Gris (*gris* means "gray") has been known to produce wines that range from white to lightly tinged pink.

Pinot Gris is thought by many to reach its pinnacle in Alsace, where it's called Tokay Pinot Gris or Tokay d'Alsace. The grapes are harvested from thirty-year-old vines and turned into a full-bodied, fruity, and creamy wine with a rich gold color.

That's a far cry from what most people know as Italy's Pinot Grigio—often a light (some might say thin), pale, and herbal wine for easy quaffing. Some of the best Pinot Grigios come from the Friuli region of Italy, where leading producers show full, rounded versions.

The current hot spot for Pinot Gris is Oregon. It was introduced there in 1966 and has become the state's premier white grape. Oregon producers prefer the name Pinot Gris to Pinot Grigio, although there's no single style of wine made: Some winemakers use oak, while others use only stainless steel. Most produce a completely dry wine, but some leave a little residual sugar.

SOME GOOD BOTTLES OF PINOT GRIS

Staete Landt Pinot Gris (Marlborough, New Zealand)—$28.00

Tscheppe Possnitzberg Pinot Gris (Austria)—$21.99

Civello Pinot Gris (Oregon)—$19.99

Riesling

Before Chardonnay became the belle of the ball, there was Riesling. In the nineteenth century, Riesling was considered the best white grape variety because it produced wines of elegance. The physical and spiritual home of Riesling is Germany, where it's been grown for at least five hundred years and possibly as long as two thousand years. It thrives in the coldest vine-growing climates and has found excellent homes in Alsace, Austria, Canada, and in the northern United States, in areas of New York, Washington, Oregon, and Michigan.

Does Not Play Well with Others

Riesling is rarely blended with other grapes. It doesn't need to be. It produces wines that run the gamut from bone dry and crisp to ultrasweet and complex. Riesling is one of the few whites that have a long aging capacity, with some lasting for over twenty years. Unlike Chardonnay, which relies on winemaker interventions for its style, Riesling relies on nature for its diversity. The winemaker really has only two decisions to make: when to pick the grapes and how long to ferment the juice.

Riesling grapes take a long time to ripen and are picked at various times throughout the harvest. The stage of ripeness of the grapes roughly corresponds to the sweetness and alcohol levels of the wines. The earliest harvested grapes produce the lightest, driest wines, which are categorized as *Kabinett*. The next category up the sweetness chain is known as *Spätlese* (late picked), followed by *Auslese* (hand-picked).

Dry Riesling

Riesling is the favored grape for the sweet and acclaimed late harvest wines and ice wines. However, for table wines the preference in recent years has been for dry wines. Producers have been deliberately making Rieslings in a dry style. Rieslings are typically crisp and low in alcohol. To lower the sugar levels, winemakers extend fermentation, which also raises the alcohol content. For the resulting German wines, the labels will say *trocken* (dry) or *halbtrocken* (off-dry).

In Alsace, the French wine region across the Rhine from Germany, Rieslings are usually fermented bone dry. Compared to a German Kabinett Riesling with between 7.5 percent and 8.5 percent alcohol, an Alsatian Riesling will have at least 12 percent alcohol. Riesling is sometimes labeled as Johannisberg Riesling, Rhine Riesling, or White Riesling.

SOME TERRIFIC RIESLINGS

Hogl Loibner Vision Riesling Smaragd (Austria)—$35.00

Triple Overtime Riesling "The Goal" (Clare Valley, Australia)—$28.00

Gottelmann Riesling Kabinett Trocken Munsterer Kapellenberg (Germany)—$17.95

Messmer Riesling Kabinett Trocken Pfalz
(Germany)—$12.95

Sauvignon Blanc

Sauvignon Blanc is widely cultivated in France and California. The Loire Valley produces wines that are 100 percent Sauvignon Blanc—most notably from Sancerre and Pouilly-Fumé. You'll find them crisp and tart. In Bordeaux, Sauvignon Blanc is usually blended with Sémillon that has been aged in oak. While not the primary grape, Sauvignon Blanc plays an important part in the sweet and revered dessert wines of Sauternes.

Sauvignon Blanc came to North America in 1878 when winemaker (and California's first agricultural commissioner) Charles Wetmore acquired cuttings from the famed Château d'Yquem vineyards in Sauternes and planted them at his Cresta Blanca Winery in Livermore, California. He propagated some of the vines in his 300 acres of nursery vineyards and sold others to California winemakers, including Carl Wente. The vines thrived, and Sauvignon Blanc became an early California favorite. A postscript to the story is that Wente Brothers (as the winery was then known) produced California's first Sauvignon Blanc-labeled wine in 1933 and in 1981 purchased Cresta Blanca—making the original Wetmore vineyards part of the current Wente Vineyards property. Sauvignon Blanc is also produced successfully in Italy, Australia, South America, and—to much recent acclaim—in New Zealand.

Sauvignon Blanc's Alias

Back in the 1960s when Robert Mondavi introduced a dry style of Sauvignon Blanc, he wanted to distinguish it from the sweet version he was already producing. He called the new wine Fumé Blanc—after Pouilly-Fumé. Rather than trademark the name for his exclusive use, he permitted other winemakers to use it. Many American wineries label their Sauvignon Blanc wines Fumé Blanc. The variations in labeling cause a lot of confusion, but Sauvignon Blanc and Fumé Blanc are from the same fruit, although they often indicate Sauvignon Blanc made in very different stylistic traditions.

A SAMPLING OF SAUVIGNON BLANC FROM DIVERSE LOCATIONS

Spring Mountain Vineyard Sauvignon Blanc (Napa Valley)—$30.00

Te Awa Sauvignon Blanc (Hawke's Bay, New Zealand)—$24.00

Two Wives Sauvignon Blanc (Napa Valley)—$22.00

Watershed "Awakening" Sauvignon Blanc (Margaret River, Australia)—$22.00

Crossroads Sauvignon Blanc (Marlborough, New Zealand)—$17.00

Viognier

Viognier is no easy grape to grow. Until the vines are about fifteen, they don't give their best fruit. The plants are susceptible to all kinds of diseases and pests. Their yields are sparse and the grapes ripen irregularly.

Maybe that's why the grape was headed toward extinction. In 1965, only a few acres of Viognier remained under cultivation in Condrieu, in the grape's Rhône Valley homeland. Since then, Viognier has been making a comeback—first in Condrieu and then in the south of France in Languedoc-Roussillon and Provence. Later, the plantings spread to California and Australia. To give you an idea of the escalation, in 1993 California crushed 231 tons of Viognier grapes. Ten years later it increased to 9,800 tons.

A Gift of Flowers and Perfume

Viognier is aromatic with vibrant floral qualities, sometimes even perfumelike. The classic Old World style of Viognier is crisp, dry, and intense. As winemakers around the world craft their own Viogniers, more variations in style appear. While cooler regions of California produce a style closer to the French classic, wines from warmer areas are richer and fuller.

It's rare for France to permit using a white wine grape in a high-quality red wine. In an unusual twist in the vineyards of the Côte-Rôtie, Viognier vines are planted among Syrah vines. The white and red grapes are harvested and vinified together to produce the highly regarded Côte-Rôtie red wines. In this same tradition, Storybook Mountain Vineyards blends a touch of Viognier in some of its Zinfandels!

SEDUCTIVE VIOGNIERS

Protero Viognier (Australia)—$38.00

Zacherle Viognier (Napa Valley)—$26.00

Up-and-Comers

Grape varieties go in and out of fashion. Or they'll be popular in one part of the world and then somehow catch on elsewhere. As Americans have tired of ordering the same old familiar varietals, they've looked for excitement in new grapes.

Grüner Veltliner

Austria has jumped onto the American scene with its dry, crisp Grüner Veltliner. It's the most extensively grown grape variety in Austria, accounting for 37 percent of all vine plantings. The wine has different expressions depending on how the grapes are grown and how they're treated by the winemaker.

Grüner Veltliner used to be treated as a high-production commercial grape. The high-yield grapes produced light and refreshing sippers that were popular in Austria's *heurigen* (wine taverns). In the 1980s Austria's wine industry made a conscious step toward higher quality. With lower yields and higher ripeness, the resulting wines are more complex and fuller flavored. The wines have a peppery quality and naturally high acidity. The best bottles of Grüner Veltliner have potential for some aging.

TASTE OF AUSTRIA:

Gritsch Axpoint Grüner Veltliner Federspiel (Wachau, Austria)—$12.00

Fiano

Italy's Campania wine region, the area around Naples and Mount Vesuvius, is the current rage. Fiano is the trendy grape. Hardly new, Fiano's history—and popularity—date back to ancient Rome. While the origin of the word is the subject of conjecture, *Fiano* may have come from "apiano" because the ripe grapes attracted bees (*apis* in Latin).

The towns of Avellino and Lapio and their surrounding areas are the primary growing centers, hence the wines are called Fiano di Avellino and Fiano di Lapio. They can be fairly light and dry with a creamy texture or (when the grapes are harvested late and fully fermented) full-bodied and ripe.

Albariño

Albariño presents certain roadblocks to its producers. Even though it's of a high quality (perhaps a relative of Riesling), it's low yielding. And its skins are so thick that only a small amount of juice can be squeezed out. Albariño's scarcity made it one of Spain's most expensive wine grapes.

In the mid-1980s only five commercial wineries existed in the Rias Baixas region of northwest Spain where Albariño is produced, so very little Albariño was made. Since then, the number of wineries has multiplied to one hundred—with a positive (if not overwhelming) effect on production. Albariño is produced across the border in Portugal, where it's called Alvarinho.

The wine has a creamy texture with complex flavors of apricots, peaches, and citrus. Albariño is rarely barrel fermented—so the flavors are clean and vibrant. In spite of its high acidity, Albariño doesn't age well and should be consumed within the first two years.

TEST THE WATERS WITH THESE QUALITY PRODUCERS

Morgadío (Spain) Albariño—$19

Valminor (Spain) Albariño—$16

Varanda do Conde (Portugal) Vino Verde Alvarinho—$11

CHAPTER 7

Pop the Bubbly!

Champagne rings in each new year, launches mighty ships, and celebrates newlyweds' vows. Bubbles are consumed to commemorate auspicious occasions—from royal coronations and corporate mergers to the birth of a child. Sparkling wine is synonymous with celebration. More and more, it's become a partner to everyday events too. Bubblies come by different names, in lots of styles, and from places far removed from France. The informed wine drinker knows how to choose the right one for any occasion.

Champagne Versus Sparkling Wine

What's the big deal? Who cares whether you call it Champagne or sparkling wine? The French do! They've protected the name *Champagne* by international treaty—which means, technically, only sparkling wines produced in the Champagne region of France can bear the name on the label. The treaty, by the way, doesn't apply in the United States.

The term *Champagne* is generically used in the United States to imply all bubblies. A hundred years ago Korbel used *Champagne* on its labels, and so have others. Only in the last few decades has France actively sought to protect the name. So American marketers, with a century of tradition behind them, continue to call their product Champagne. And most people—wine geeks included—do the same. Technically, however, Champagne only comes from the region of its namesake in France, and all other bubblies are sparkling wines.

Making the Bubbles

Champagne is more than a name. It's a universally adored beverage whose bubbles are created in a time-consuming and labor-intensive process. The technique, *méthode champenoise*, has six basic steps:

1. Grapes are fermented for about three weeks to produce still wines.
2. The producer blends still wines according to what style he or she wants to achieve. This base wine is called the cuvée.
3. The wine is bottled and laid down. During the next nine weeks or so, a second fermentation takes place inside the bottle—producing carbon dioxide in the form of bubbles.
4. The wine is aged—anywhere from nine months to several years—according to the producer's specifications.

5. The bottles are rotated from a horizontal position to a vertical, upside-down position. This allows sediment to collect in the neck of the bottle close to the cork so that it can be removed easily and quickly. Rotating the bottles is called riddling.

6. The neck of the bottle is frozen and the sediment (in the form of a frozen plug) is removed—called disgorging. At this point, sugar is added (a process known as dosage)—the amount dependent on how sweet the producer wants the final product—and the bottles are recorked.

Cheap Bubbles

The traditional method of producing bubbles is expensive. The price you pay is a reflection of that. You can bet that when you buy a $5 bottle of sparkling wine, it was produced another—cheaper—way. The Charmat method (also known as bulk method, tank method, and cuve close) was likely used. It involves conducting the second fermentation in large, closed, pressurized tanks. With this process, you can produce a lot of wine in a short period of time, so the sparkling wine is ready to drink not long after harvest, sometimes in only a few weeks. Here's what happens:

1. Still wine is put into closed, pressurized tanks, and sugar and yeast are added.

2. Fermentation takes place and carbon dioxide forms in the wine, producing a sparkling wine with an alcohol content higher than the base wine.

3. The wine is filtered under pressure to remove any solids.

4. Sugar is added to adjust to the sweetness level desired, and the wine is bottled.

An even less expensive technique simply injects carbon dioxide into the wine—like a carbonated soft drink. If that's the case, the label on the bottle will say "carbonated."

The Grapes Matter

To be real Champagne, only three grape varieties are allowed: Pinot Meunier, Pinot Noir, and Chardonnay. Pinot Meunier contributes a youthful fruitiness; Pinot Noir gives Champagne its weight, richness, and longevity.

One of the most important decisions for the maker of Champagne is how to blend these grapes to make the base wine. Wines from the different varieties and vineyards are kept separate. The producer then blends the wines (including wines from past years) in varying proportions to create its distinct cuvée. This is what distinguishes the ultimate taste of one producer's Champagne compared to others.

For sparkling wines produced by other methods, there are no such strict rules regarding grape variety. Generally speaking, tank-fermented bubblies tend to be fruitier than their *méthode champenoise* counterparts.

Thirsty for Knowledge?

There are a range of neat technological devices vineyard managers and winemakers use to measure the sugar content of a grape, or its brix, before harvest. One of the biggest treats on a trip to wine country is walking through a vineyard with the vineyard manager or winemaker, hearing about which tools he or she uses and what ultimately motivates the decision to harvest. While much of the decision is motivated by science (brix, expected weather patterns), you will be wonderfully amazed that the final decision still comes down to experience and intuition.

Champagne Through the Years

Until the mid-1600s, Champagne as we know it didn't exist. The region produced still wines, which were very popular with European nobility. The Champagne region in northern France has a cold climate, which posed problems for growing grapes and winemaking since the short growing season meant that grapes had to be harvested as late as possible for optimum ripeness. That resulted in less time for the must to ferment, since the cold temperatures of winter would put an end to the process. Therefore, the wines were bottled before all the sugar had been converted to alcohol.

Then spring would arrive, and fermentation would begin again—this time in the bottle. If the bottles didn't explode from all the pressure that had built up from the carbon dioxide inside, the wines would often have bubbles. To the winemakers of the time, bubbles were a sign of poor winemaking.

Dom Pérignon, the Benedictine monk often credited with the invention of Champagne, was one of those winemakers. He spent a good deal of time trying to prevent the bubbles. He wasn't successful, but he did develop the basic principles used in Champagne making that continue to this day:

- He advanced the art of blending to include different grapes and different vineyards of the same grape.
- He invented a method to produce white juice from black grapes.
- He improved clarification techniques.
- He used stronger bottles to prevent exploding.

When Dom Pérignon died in 1715, Champagne accounted for only about 10 percent of the region's wine, but it was fast becoming the preferred drink of English and French royalty. A royal ordinance in 1735 dictated the size, weight, and shape of Champagne bottles as well as the size of the cork. Two historic Champagne houses came into existence: Ruinart in 1729 and Moët in 1743. By the 1800s the Champagne industry was in full swing.

Champagne Houses? Sounds Great!

Unlike other French wines that are named after growing regions, Champagnes are named for the houses that produce them. The houses, in turn, produce various brands of Champagne—called marques. The largest and most famous of the houses are known as Grandes Marques, which translates to, you guessed it, big brands! Twenty-four of them belong to an organization that requires they meet certain minimum standards. Some of the more recognizable members are:

- Charles Heidsieck
- Krug
- Laurent-Perrier
- Louis Roederer
- Moët & Chandon
- G. H. Mumm
- Perrier-Jouët
- Pol Roger
- Pommery
- Ruinart
- Taittinger
- Veuve Clicquot Ponsardin

Beginning with Moët & Chandon in 1974, a number of French Champagne houses opened up shop in California. They produce sparkling wines the traditional way using the same grape varieties as in France: Pinot Noir, Chardonnay, and Pinot Meunier. The French-American productions include Domaine Carneros (owned by Taittinger),

Domaine Chandon (owned by Moët & Chandon), Mumm Cuvée Napa (owned by G. H. Mumm), Piper Sonoma (owned by Piper-Heidsieck), and Roederer Estate (owned by Louis Roederer).

Grower Champagne

While some of the major Champagne houses have size-able vineyard holdings, they still buy most of their grapes from the 20,000 or so small growers in the Champagne district. The small growers, who collectively own about 90 percent of the vineyards, are increasingly making their own Champagnes. About 130 of these grower Champagnes are available in the U.S. market (out of the 3,747 sold in France). You've probably never heard their names (they can't afford to pay for promotion and advertising like the big guys), but they offer high quality and bargain prices.

How do you recognize a grower Champagne? It's on the label. In the lower right-hand corner of the front label are two letters followed by some numbers. The letters that indicate a grower Champagne are either "RM" or "SR." (See Chapter 4 for more on reading Champagne labels.) Here are all the possible letter-codes and what they mean:

NM (*négociant-manipulant*)—The term means merchant-distributor. These are the big houses. They buy grapes in volume from independent growers.

RM (*récoltant-manipulant*)—The term means grower-distributor. This is a grower that makes and markets its own Champagne.

SR (*société de récoltants*)—This is basically the same as grower Champagne. Two or more growers share a winemaking facility and market their own brands.

CM (*coopérative de manipulation*)—This is a coop-erative of growers who bottle their product together, although these wines can include purchased grapes.

RC (*récoltant-coopérateur*)—This means a grower sends its grapes to a cooperative to be made into wine. The grapes can be blended with other wines in the cooperative.

Need Help Choosing That Bottle of Bubbly?

A Champagne house establishes its reputation based on a particular style. Many factors influence the style—grape varieties, vineyards, blending choices, tradition. The objective of each house is to provide consistency from one year to the next. When you find a Champagne that you like, you can be sure it will have the same character-istics year after year.

BOTTLENOTES' FAVORITE CHAMPAGNE

Taittinger Prelude Grands Crus Champagne—$67.00

Vintage Years

Champagne is produced every year. "Vintage" Cham-pagnes are only produced in the best years. Like in all other regions, some grape harvests in Champagne are better than others. In exceptional years, a house will decide to make its bubbly using only the grapes from that harvest and will date the bottle with that year. In the years in between, the house blends wines from multiple years, and this Champagne is termed *non-vintage* (NV). Blending across years is one reason you can expect uni-form quality.

Non-vintage Champagne represents 80 percent or more of a house's production. They're usually lighter, fresher, and less complex than their vintage counterparts.

From Dry to Sweet

If Champagne were like most other wines, the grapes would be picked when perfectly ripe. They'd have plenty of natural sugar to be converted to alcohol. Alas, that's not the case, and the less-than-ripe grapes need additional sugar so the yeast will have adequate fuel to convert into alcohol. The amount of sugar is left to the discretion of the winemaker—the more sugar, the sweeter the Champagne. There's another addition of sweetness at the end of the process right before bottling. Sweetness levels of Champagne are important parts of their styles. Progressing from dry to sweet, these are the levels:

Extra brut (also called brut sauvage, ultra brut, brut integral, brut zero)—driest of all but not a common style

Brut—the most popular style and considered to be a good balance of sweetness to dryness

Extra dry (or extra sec)—dry to medium-dry

Sec—medium-dry to medium-sweet

Demi-sec—sweet

Doux—very sweet

Variations on a Theme

Pink, or Rosé, Champagne conjures ideas of quintessential romance! Rosé Champagne gets its pink color in one of two ways. The winemaker can leave the skins of the grapes in brief contact with the grape juice during the first fermentation, or add a little Pinot Noir wine to base the wine blend. People sometimes think of Rosé Champagne as sweet (maybe because they associate it with sweet blush wines), but it's definitely dry, often brut. It's available both as a vintage wine and as non-vintage.

Blanc de noir has a hint of pink too. In wine terms, *blanc de noir* means "white wine from black grapes." This Champagne is made from just one of the permitted grapes: Pinot Noir or, less often, Pinot Meunier. It's fuller than Champagnes with Chardonnay in the blend. *Blanc de blanc* is another one-grape bubbly, made entirely from Chardonnay. It's lighter and more delicate than Champagnes that also include Pinot Noir.

Name Your Size

Have you ever noticed those super-large Champagne bottles on display at wine stores and restaurants? Well, they're not just some marketing tool. They're real. Champagne is bottled in ten different sizes, shown in the following table.

CHAMPAGNE BOTTLE SIZES AND NAMES

Measure	Size Equivalent	Servings	Popular Name
187 ml	quarter bottle	1	split
375 ml	half bottle	2	half
750 ml	standard	4	fifth
1.5 L	2 bottles	8	magnum
3 L	4 bottles	17	jeroboam
4.5 L	6 bottles	24	rehoboam
6 L	8 bottles	34	methuselah
9 L	12 bottles	50	salmanazar
12 L	16 bottles	68	balthazar
15 L	20 bottles	112	nebuchadnezzar

Only the half bottle, standard bottle, and magnum contain Champagne that has undergone the second fermentation in the bottle. And the three largest sizes are rarely made anymore. How many people must it take to pour from them?

Champagne by Any Other Name

The fact that a sparkling wine is produced outside of the Champagne region of France doesn't mean that it's inferior. It's just a little different. Some sparklers are made with the exact same grapes employing the same traditional method. They'll be different because of the terroir—the taste the earth has given to the grapes—and the blending choices of the winemaker. But even some experts have failed to recognize the difference between well-made bubblies from inside and outside the Champagne region.

French but Not Champagne

Even in the Loire Valley (close to Champagne) they can't use the Champagne name on the labels of their sparkling wines. The region, known in part for its use of Chenin Blanc grapes in Vouvray, uses the same grapes for its bubblies. The effect is refreshing and creamy.

The eastern regions of France, including Alsace, are known for blending Pinot Noir, Pinot Blanc, and Pinot Gris into their crisp sparkling wines. French sparkling wines produced outside of Champagne are labeled "Vins Mousseux."

Spanish Bubbly

It used to be called "Spanish Champagne," but in 1970 the European Union banned the use of the term outside of Champagne. From then on Spanish sparkling wines have been known as *Cava*. The word is Catalan for "cellar," referring to the underground cellars where the wines are aged.

To qualify as a Cava, the sparkling wine has to be produced in the traditional method using specified grape varieties. The list includes Chardonnay and Pinot Noir, which are used in the best wines, but producers still use the big three indigenous grapes: Macabeo, Xarel-Lo, and Parellada. Cavas are usually light and crisp. Look for:

Cav Vendrell Brut Cava—$19.99

Italian Sparklers

Oh, so many bubblies to choose from in Italy . . . starting with Prosecco. It's made from the grape of the same name in the Veneto region of northeastern Italy. Prosecco comes both fully sparkling *(spumante)* and lightly sparkling *(frizzante)*. They're crisp and dry and inexpensive. They've become very popular, and you see more and more of them on restaurant wine lists.

BOTTLENOTES' FAVORITE PROSECCO

La Tordera Prosecco (Valdobbiadene, Italy)—$14.50

Then there's the more familiar Asti (in the past known as Asti Spumante) made from the Muscat grape. Its second fermentation takes place in pressurized tanks in a modified version of the Charmat method, and its taste is semisweet to sweet. Asti's cousin is Moscato d'Asti. It differs from Asti in that it's frizzante instead of fully sparkling, sweeter, lower in alcohol, and is corked like a still wine. Both should be drunk young and fresh.

Moscato d'Asti DOCG "Badis"—$20.00

Lambrusco is another Italian option. Most Americans know it as pink, semisweet, and frizzante, but it's also made white and dry.

Domestic Sparkling Wine

Sparkling wine is made almost everywhere still wine is made—the two largest producing states being California and New York. In California, particularly in the cooler climates of Sonoma and Mendocino Counties, many wineries (not just the ones with ties to France) produce excellent bubblies. Names to look for: Gloria Ferrer, Iron Horse, and Schramsberg, to name just a few. While California gets most of the attention, sparkling wine has been a mainstay of New York winemaking since before the Civil War when French Champagne-makers were recruited there by local wineries. Some sparkling wine recommendations from around the United States:

Iron Horse Vineyards Blanc de Blancs—$37.00

Schramsberg Brut Rosé—$32.00

J Vineyards "Cuvée 20" NV—$30.00

Gloria Ferrer Blancs de Noirs—$14.99

Storing and Serving in Your Own Home

You never know when you'll need a bottle of Champagne. A friend drops in to say he or she has gotten (pick one) engaged, divorced, promoted, a raise, a diploma, a puppy. You need an appropriate way to celebrate: Champagne. Or you get home after a long day of arguing with your boss. You need an effective mood enhancer: Champagne. It's the universal beverage. Keeping a supply just makes good sense.

How to Keep It When You're Not Drinking It

Champagne is sensitive to temperature and light. Like other wines, it does best stored in a cool, dark place without big temperature fluctuations. The same 52–57°F rule as for still wine applies. Champagne is ready for immediate consumption as soon as it leaves the Champagne house, but if you provide the right conditions for your bubbly, it'll last for three to four years—if you haven't drunk it by then.

Don't be afraid to keep it in the refrigerator. A couple of weeks in the cold isn't going to hurt it.

Bubbly is best served around 45°F. It will take three to four hours in the refrigerator to cool a bottle, but you can quick-chill your Champagne in about twenty minutes by immersing the bottle in ice water, which is faster than ice alone. Half ice and half water in an ice bucket is the way to go. No bucket? The kitchen sink will do.

Popping the Cork

First word of advice: Popping the cork wastes bubbles. The cork should be removed so the sound you hear is a soft sigh. Removing the cork in this slow manner also reduces the risks of killing someone in the room. (After all, there are 70 pounds per square inch of pressure in that bottle!) Here's a checklist for how to safely open your bottle of Champagne:

1. Remove the foil covering.
2. Stand the bottle on a counter for support. (It's safer than holding the bottle in your arms and possibly pointing it at someone.)
3. Get a towel. Keep one hand over the top of the cork with the towel between your hand and the cork. Untwist the wire cage. Remove the wire.
4. Keep the towel on top of the cork with one hand and put your other hand on the bottle at a point where you have a good grasp.
5. Turn the bottle—not the cork. You'll feel the cork loosen a bit. Keep a downward pressure on the cork until it completely loosens and finally releases.
6. Hold the cork over the opened bottle for a few seconds to ensure that as little carbon dioxide escapes as possible. Contrary to popular opinion, the less noise and mess a Champagne makes when uncorked the better.

7. Pour! Pour slowly. Because of the bubbles, the liquid rises quickly, and you can end up with overflow (and wasted Champagne!) before you know it.

Drinking Vessels

You've undoubtedly seen the sherbet-style glasses that were popular in the 1950s. Now that retro is so chic, the glasses are everywhere. Buy them if you want, but don't use them for Champagne. Long-stemmed flutes are the glassware of choice for sparkling wines. The elongated shape and slight narrowing at the rim enhance the flow of bubbles and keep them from escaping.

There's no need to chill the glasses. If you do, they'll just fog up and cloud your view of the bubbles.

Speaking of glasses, if there's soap residue on the glasses, you may experience lots of foam that doesn't subside. This is caused when the carbon dioxide meets the detergent. To prevent this, always rinse the glasses thoroughly when they're washed. And dusty glasses will destroy the bubbles.

BOTTLENOTES' RECOMMENDED SPARKLING WINE FLUTE

Bottega del Vino "Champagner"—$40.00/flute

How to Use Your Champagne Leftovers

On the rare occasions that the bottle of bubbly hasn't been emptied, your main objective is to save the bubbles for another day. Your best bet to preserve the effervescence is a Champagne bottle stopper. It's made of metal with a spring and special lip to grab the rim of the bottle. They're available in most kitchen stores, as well as in wine stores in states that allow them to sell wine accessories. A good backup procedure is to wrap the bottle opening with two layers of plastic wrap and secure it with a rubber band.

Alas! You open the refrigerator door, and all the bubbles have disappeared. There are still last-ditch efforts you can make to try to revive the wine, even if they sound a little silly. One is to put a raisin in the bottle. Another is to put a paper clip into the bottom of each glass before you pour the Champagne into them. It's always worth a try. Remember, even without bubbles, Champagne makes an excellent cooking wine!

CHAPTER 8

And for Dessert . . .

To paraphrase Shakespeare, "A dessert wine by any other name would taste as sweet." In the United States "dessert wine" means fortified wines—both sweet and dry. In Australia, dessert wines are called "stickies." Elsewhere in the world, dessert wines refer to sweet wines in general. By whatever name, they've recently become the darlings of the wine world—with prices to match.

Sweet Wines and Their Rich History

The popularity of sweet wines has gone through cycles: One day they're on top of the heap, the next they're out of favor. Some of them were almost accidents of nature. Others were more accidents of commerce. Whatever their origins, they've had a resurgence in popularity of late.

Sweet wines go back to ancient times. The most acclaimed wines in Rome were sweet and white. The ancient winemakers either let the grapes raisin on the vine or dried them on straw mats to concentrate their flavors. The resulting wines were sweeter and stronger—and more durable, able to withstand transportation to outlying areas.

In the Middle Ages, Venice and Genoa made sweet dried-grape wines that they exported to northern Europe. Sweet wines appeared in other parts of the world too. Tokaji from Hungary and Constantia from South Africa were highly prized sweet wines that were on every royal table in Europe.

Explaining a Late Harvest and Noble Rot

Legends, by definition, aren't totally reliable, but here's one version of the creation of late harvest sweet wines: In 1775 a messenger was sent to Schloss Johannisberg in Germany's Rheingau region to give the official order to start harvesting the grapes. He was robbed on the way and delayed. By the time he got to the wine estate, the grapes had begun to raisin on the vine. They were picked anyway and produced astonishingly delicious sweet wine. There's evidence that sweet late harvest wines had already been produced throughout Europe in the previous century, but it makes for a colorful story.

Late Harvest Wines

The term *late harvest* means that the grapes were picked late into the harvest season when they were ripened past the sugar levels required for ordinary table wine. The extra ripening time—which can be weeks—adds sugar but also adds significant risk from rain, rot, and birds. The high sugar content of the grapes can translate into a wine that's sweet or a wine high in alcohol—or both.

Late harvest wines are known for their rich, honeyed flavors. Riesling grapes (the variety of most late harvest wines) have the ability to develop high sugar levels and, at the same time, maintain their acidity. That's why they can be unbelievably sweet without also being cloying. The acidity also helps these white wines to age as well as they do. Late harvest wines aren't limited to Riesling, as they're also made from Sauvignon Blanc, Gewürztraminer, Sémillon, and Zinfandel.

Noble Rot

The French have their own legend for the famous Sauternes wines. It seems a château owner told his workers not to pick his grapes until he got back from a trip. By the time he returned, the grapes were infected with a fungus that shriveled them. Despite their disgusting appearance, the grapes were picked and turned into wine. The taste was so exquisite that the owner declared his grapes would thereafter always be picked after the fungus had arrived.

The friendly fungus of the legend is *Botrytis cinerea*, known affectionately as noble rot. It helps the water in the grape evaporate, causing the grape to shrivel and leaving a more concentrated sweet juice. A wide range of grapes can benefit from the positive effects of noble rot—Riesling, Chenin Blanc, Gewürztraminer, Sauvignon Blanc, Sémillon, and Furmint among them. Three areas in particular are historically famous for their botrytized wines.

Sauternes—The wine by the same name is made mostly from Sémillon but usually includes some Sauvignon Blanc and sometimes Muscadelle. The sweet Sauternes aren't necessarily made every year. If the grapes don't ripen properly and if botrytis infection doesn't set in, the winemakers may decide to produce dry wines instead and label them as Bordeaux.

Germany—German winemakers use Riesling to produce their Beerenauslese and Trockenbeerenauslese wines.

Hungary—Tokaji (also referred to as Tokay) comes from an area around the town of Tokaj. They're made primarily from Furmint grapes.

Ice Wines Can Warm You Up!

Making wine from frozen grapes was one of those divine accidents. The discovery of ice wine dates back to the winter of 1794 when producers in Franconia, Germany, had frozen grapes on their hands and decided to go forward with the pressing. When they finished, they were startled by the high sugar concentration of the juice.

When grapes freeze, their water contents forms ice. As the grapes are crushed, the ice is left behind with the other solids—the skins and seeds. To give you an idea of how concentrated the juice is: If the sugar content of the juice was 22 percent when pressed normally, it would be 50 percent or more after freezing and pressing.

In order for the grapes to freeze, they have to be left on the vine well into the winter months. Waiting for them to freeze can be a risky business. If the weather doesn't cooperate and the grapes don't freeze, a grower can lose his or her entire crop. Harvesting takes place by hand in the early (and necessarily cold) morning hours when acidity levels are at their highest. Pressing produces only tiny amounts of juice—one reason for the extremely high prices of ice wines.

Who Makes Ice Wine

Germany and Austria were the traditional producers of ice wine (*Eiswein* in German), but in the last ten years Canada has taken over as the largest producer. Canadian winters are much more predictable. The Canadian versions use a variety of grapes besides Riesling, including some lesser-known varieties like Vidal Blanc and Vignoles.

In Canada—as in Germany and Austria—the making of ice wines is strictly regulated. There are standards for sugar levels, temperature at harvest, and processing. Ice wines are also produced in the United States—particularly in Washington State, New York's Finger Lakes region, and states around the Great Lakes like Michigan and Ohio where no such strict standards exist.

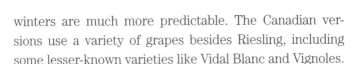

Thirsty for Knowledge?

Some producers use an alternate method for making ice wine: They stick the grapes in the freezer before pressing them. The lower prices for these ice wines reflect the easier method of production. It's a less risky method, but it's also untraditional. We at Bottlenotes don't discriminate based on method, but we do discriminate based on taste! We'll leave you to decide if the natural method is worth the higher price.

Serving Ice Wine

Ice wines and sweet late harvest wines come in small (375 ml) bottles with big price tags. It isn't unusual to pay $60 to $200 for a half bottle. Fortunately, you serve less of them—two to three ounces—than you would a table wine. They're best served chilled (45° Fahrenheit).

BOTTLENOTES' RECOMMENDED ICE WINES

Peninsula Ridge Icewine 2005 (Niagara Peninsula, Canada)—$54.00

Weir Vidal Icewine 2005 (Niagara Peninsula, Canada)—$56.00

Port—Only Gets Better with Age

The origins of Port—the great fortified red wine—go back to the seventeenth-century trade wars between England and France. The British had developed a real affection for the wines of Bordeaux, but import bans and high taxes forced the English merchants to look elsewhere for their red wines. That elsewhere was Portugal. They found wines to their liking inland along the Douro River. To make sure that the wines arrived back in England in good condition, the merchants added brandy to stabilize them before shipping them. In 1678, a Liverpool wine merchant sent his sons to Portugal to search out some wines. They ended up at a monastery in the mountains above the Douro where the abbot was adding brandy during fermentation—not after. The alcohol stopped the fermentation process, leaving a sweet, high-alcohol wine. That, as legend has it, was the beginning of Port as the world has come to know it.

What's in a Name

English merchants set up trading companies in the city of Oporto to ship the wines to England. That's one reason so many of the Port producers have English names. The wine became known as Porto, and to this day that designation on the label means that the contents are authentic Port. Similar to the rules about Champagne, to be called Port the wine has to come from a specific place—the Douro region of Portugal. Port-style wines are made all over the world, but they're not true Port. The regulations governing Port's production allow eighty different grape varieties to be used. In practice, though, it really comes down to a handful. The most important ones are:

- Tinta Roriz (the same as Spain's Tempranillo)
- Touriga Nacional
- Tinta Barroca
- Tinto Cão
- Touriga Francesca

- Bastardo
- Mourisco

Ports come in a head-spinning number of styles. While most of them are red and sweet, not all are. The style varies according to the quality of the base wine, how long the wine ages in wood before it's bottled, and whether the wine is from a single year or blended with wines from other years.

Port is aged in large wooden casks over a number of years. It reacts with oxygen through the surface area and the wooden stoves. The aging process in bottles is much slower because there's almost no oxygen. Ports are either wood Ports or bottle-aged Ports—except when they're a little bit of both. Is all this becoming perfectly clear?

Top of the Line: Vintage Port

A vintage Port is aged in the bottle for most of its life. It spends only two years in the cask. When it's bottled at the age of two, it hasn't had a chance to shed its harsh tannins. That's left to happen in the bottle, which—without oxygen—is going to take a very long time. It requires at least twenty years of aging and can continue to improve for decades after that. What really distinguishes a vintage Port from all the others is that the grapes come from the best vineyard sites in a singularly outstanding year. And that doesn't occur every year. On average a vintage Port will be made three years out of ten. The wines that are produced in the off ("undeclared") years go into the other types of Port. Vintage Port is bottled unfiltered and unfined, so once opened it requires decanting to remove the sediment that has accumulated. The wine should be consumed in one sitting.

Late-Bottled Vintage Port (LBV)

LBVs are probably the next best thing to vintage Port. They're vintage dated and made from a producer's best grapes, but they come from undeclared years. LBVs spend from five to six years in the cask to speed up the aging process. They're ready to drink when they're released.

Tawny Port

Tawnies are aged in wood for years—as many as forty—until they fade to a tawny color. They're a blend of wines from several years and are ready to drink immediately. Once opened, they can retain their vitality for a few weeks.

A Tawny Port will often be categorized by age, which appears as "10 Year Old," "20 Year Old," "30 Year Old," and "40 Year Old" on the label. The number is really an average age because older, more complex wines are blended with younger, fruitier wines. Colheita Ports are Tawny Ports from a single year (*colheita* is Portuguese for "vintage").

Ruby Port

Ruby Port is one of the least expensive Ports. It's bottled while it's still young—with only two to three years in wood. It retains its dark ruby color and has a limited shelf life. "Reserve" or "Special Reserve" indicates it's been aged longer.

White Port

White Port is produced just like red Port except it's made from white grapes—principally Malvasia and Donzelinho. Producers sometimes make a drier style by lengthening the fermentation period. The drier whites are typically served as an apéritif.

RECOMMENDED PORTS

Zacherle Knights Valley Port NV (Sonoma County)— $90.00 (750 ml)

St. Barthelemy Petite Sirah Port (Napa Valley)— $20.00

Broadbent Auction Reserve Porto NV (Portugal)—
$21.75

Sherry—Overlooked and Underpriced?

Say "Sherry," and you immediately think of England.
Sherry comes from Spain and is the underrated and
misunderstood fortified wine. It's produced in the Jerez
region from three main grape varieties: Palomino for the
dry Sherries and Pedro Jimenex and Moscatel for the
sweet wines. Making Sherry involves a number of steps
and many twists and turns.

Relying on a Finicky Yeast

Once the base wine is made and put into barrels, a yeast
called *flor* forms on the top of the wine. Not all the wines
in the barrels are susceptible to the yeast, and the yeast
will only grow with proper temperature and humidity. The
flor does a couple of things. It influences the flavor—adding a tangy character to the wine—and it creates a protec-
tive layer, like a crust, on top of the wine so no further oxidation can occur. How well the flor develops determines
the style of the Sherry. When the flor fully forms, the wine
will be dry and crisp. These will be *fino* Sherry.

Occasionally—and mysteriously—the flor will begin to
form and then stop. This may happen in one out of every
hundred barrels. The dry and complex Sherry that results
is called Palo Cortado.

Wines that don't form the flor at all are the *olorosos*,
which have a rich, raisin flavor. They develop with full
exposure to the air.

Fortifying and Blending

The next step is to fortify the wines with a clear
Brandy, which boosts their alcohol content—and then on
to one of the most fascinating blending operations in all
of winemaking, known as the *solera system*. Since most

Sherries aren't vintage dated, there is a need to make the wines consistent from year to year. To achieve this, wines from many years—and sometimes wines from as far back as a hundred years—are blended together.

Imagine rows and rows of casks all stacked on top of each other—up to fourteen tiers. The oldest wines are on the bottom and the youngest are on top. Producers remove from a quarter to a third of the wine from the bottom barrels and bottle it. They replace what they just removed with a wine from the next oldest, one tier up. This cascading of Sherry from the younger to the older continues all the way to the top. By blending all these wines together, you get a product that's consistent and homogenous.

Sherry to the nth Power

Sherries start out as either a fino or an oloroso (with the very few exceptions of the Palo Cortado). Then it gets complicated. Sometimes aging will change the character of a Sherry so it no longer fits into its initial category. Sometimes the Sherries are sweetened, producing even more different styles. Among the sweet Sherries are:

Paul-Cream—a lightly sweetened fino

Cream Sherry—a heavily sweetened oloroso

Brown Sherry—an extremely sweet and dark oloroso

Madeira—How Heat Helps Flavor

Madeira is just about indestructible. While almost all other wines can't take heat and motion and won't last more than a couple of days once the bottles are opened, Madeira can survive all those things. In fact, Madeira thrives on heat. That's how it's made.

Madeira is a Portuguese island off the coast of North Africa. It was perfectly situated in the Atlantic to become a thriving port for ships traveling to South America and around Africa to Asia. Ships loaded wine onboard for the long journeys. The only problem was that the wines were undrinkable by the time the ships arrived at their destinations. So alcohol, distilled from cane sugar, was added to stabilize the wines. After enough trips, it was discovered that the wines tasted better after the voyages than before and that Madeira that had made a roundtrip was better than Madeira that had traveled only one way. Shippers began putting wine in the holds of ships for the sole purpose of developing their flavors. It eventually got too expensive, so winemakers had to come up with other ways to simulate the journeys. Subjecting the wine to heat did the trick.

Madeira usually starts out as a white wine. After fermentation it spends at least three months in heated tanks or rooms—or exposed to the sun. As the wine bakes, sugars become caramelized to an amber color, and the wine is oxidized. The term is *maderized*. The different styles of Madeira are named after the grapes they're made from:

Sercial—the driest style, tangy with high acidity

Verhelho—medium-dry with nutty flavor

Bual (or Boal)—rich, medium-sweet with raisin flavor

Malvasia (or Malmsy)—sweet and concentrated

Sercial and Verdelho are appropriate as apéritifs. The sweeter two are dessert wines. When grape names don't appear on the label, the style will be indicated in a more straightforward fashion: dry, medium-dry, medium-sweet, and sweet.

RECOMMENDED MADEIRAS

Broadbent Malmsey 10 Years Old White Wine Madeira NV (Portugal)—$46.00

Broadbent Direct Colhetia Sweet Red Wine Madeira 1996 (Portugal)—$45.00

Part 2

Around the World in 80 Sips, from West to East

Now that we have discussed an array of grape varieties, the history of wine, and how wine is made, it's time to examine the different regions of the wine-producing world. This is not an exhaustive list—just the regions that we at Bottlenotes tend to enjoy most frequently.

NAPA

Key Tastes

Cabernet Sauvignon, Merlot, Red Meritages (Bordeaux blends), Zinfandel, Sauvignon Blanc, Chardonnay, Syrah

Napa Valley Cabs often boast big and powerful flavors, including, but not limited to, chocolate, blackberry, and cocoa tones on the nose and midpalate.

Chardonnay from the Napa Valley is classically referred to as "oak" and "buttery." Napa Valley Chardonnay is often an extremely full and lush wine.

Meritage is the official name for a Bordeaux-style California blend with no more than 90 percent of one variety and featuring at least two of the following: Cabernet Sauvignon, Merlot, Cabernet Franc, Malbec, or Petit Verdot.

Merlot from the Napa Valley has a soft, lush, fruity character accompanied by juicy flavors of black cherry, fig, plum, prunes, and chocolate.

Sauvignon Blanc from the Napa Valley often offers subtle floral or citrus aromas and boasts crisp acidity.

Zinfandel is the only grape variety indigenous to California. California Zins are often described as jammy and offer concentrated fruit flavors and a good helping of spice.

Syrah is the next hot grape variety from Napa Valley, one that many Napa Valley winemakers are playing with as personal projects. Napa Valley Syrahs offer the classic pepper on the nose (sometimes black pepper, sometimes white) and in general are big and powerful, and jammy, wines with an attractive spiciness.

Napa Valley often doubles as the face of California wine. Representing the pinnacle of achievement of New

World wines, Napa boasts the best reputation and highest prices of any region in California. The temperate location, sandwiched between California's cool coastline and the hot Central Valley, is ideal for winemaking. As a result, life in the valley revolves around the vines.

History

Though quite established for the United States, Napa's history with wine is brief in comparison with Bordeaux or Burgundy. Although the first wines from Napa were produced prior to the gold rush, viticulture followed the agricultural boom with the arrival of the forty-niners. The vast influx of prospectors flooded the state with consumers, and farmers quickly increased production due to their demands.

Enterprising settlers quickly realized that the benefits of making wine—a necessary supply for the disappointed and unlucky men panning for gold—outweighed the slim chance of finding enough gold to cover one's costs. Within thirty years, Napa was producing excellent wines and the industry was booming.

The devastating effects of Prohibition lasted until the middle of the twentieth century, when the industry returned to—and surpassed—its former glory. Over the last half century, the number of wineries in Napa has increased from sixty-five to over two hundred, and the quality continues to improve. The high quality of the wines was validated by the Paris tasting of 1976 (the Judgment of Paris, see Chapter 1), when two Napa Valley wines took top honors for both red and white, thrusting the region into the very center of the international limelight.

Today Napa's wines are prized around the world, and the region's fame attracts a staggering five million visitors a year from the United States and abroad. If you're planning a trip, however, you should know that winetasting in

Napa is unfortunately no longer free. To deal with tourist traffic, wineries have taken to charging visitors to sample the wine. This practice is not followed elsewhere in California, but it is necessary here to keep the valley from being overwhelmed with cars.

Despite the high volume of tourists, the land remains unspoiled due to strict building regulations and extensive preservation efforts by the region's pioneers, such as Jack and Dolores Cakebread. Although these regulations make it difficult to start and expand wineries, they check the growth of urban sprawl and protect Napa's beauty and agricultural essence.

An Entrepreneurial Inspiration: Cakebread Cellars

Over 30 years ago, Jack Cakebread came to the Napa Valley as a photographer, one who had studied under Ansel Adams. On his way home to Oakland that afternoon, Jack stopped for lunch at the home of a family friend. There, he offered to purchase the land on which they were sitting, using the check he had received as an advance for the photo shoot as his sole deposit. While the friends accepted his offer, Dolores, Jack's wife and life-long sweetheart (since age 13!) asked him to return the next day, let the friends know he'd made a mistake, and ask for the advance back. Fortunately for us all, Dolores too fell in love with the property—and Cakebread Cellars was born.

Bottlenotes could not be more grateful for the awesome support of Jack Cakebread, one of the Fathers of Napa Valley, on our Board of Directors.

Geography

North of San Francisco, Napa is the heart of wine country, with a mild, Mediterranean climate. The large region includes several different terroirs with multiple microclimates, allowing the production of excellent warm-weather grapes, like Cabernet Sauvignon, and cool-climate grapes, such as Chardonnay or Pinot Noir. Toward the southern end of the valley, the San Pablo Bay exerts a significant cooling influence. For this reason, the southern end of the valley is mostly devoted to cool-climate grapes like Chardonnay and Pinot Noir. Further north, the bay has less of an influence and Pinot Noir thrives in the warmer climate.

Napa ranges from sea level to 2,700 feet along mountain ridges. Higher elevations are generally associated with cooler temperatures, but in Napa the maritime influence makes the situation far more complex. A hillside vineyard above the fog will probably have cooler temperatures than a sea-level vineyard during the day. When the fog rolls in at night, however, the vineyard on the valley floor becomes cooler. For this reason, hillside vineyards are better protected from frost.

Like most large wine regions, Napa includes a wide variety of soils. Unlike most regions, Napa's seismic activity is responsible for much of the present soil composition. On the valley floor the soil is heavy, with clay mixed with sand and gravel that improves drainage. Along the banks of the Napa River, silt, sand, and gravel are the norm. Napa is particularly known for the soil in the Rutherford Bench that lies above the river floodplain, which produces excellent Cabernet Sauvignon. For more information on these districts and others, visit *www.wine cyclopedia.com*.

Stags Leap District

There is a bit of confusion concerning the apostrophe in Stags Leap. The famous wine cellar is spelled "Stag's Leap," and a less famous winery is called "Stags' Leap." The name of the AVA, however, is correct without any apostrophe at all.

The soil in Stags Leap is red, gravelly, volcanic, and well drained, with warm daytime temperatures moderated by cooler temperatures at night. Stags Leap Cabernet are most closely rivaled by those from Rutherford. Stags Leap also produces excellent Merlot, Petite Sirah, and Bordeaux blends.

Wild Horse Valley

Wild Horse Valley is a part of Napa only as a technicality, as the region is actually more a part of Solano County than of Napa. The soil here is red and volcanic, and what little cultivation exists here occurs on a 1,000-foot plateau due east of the town of Napa.

Yountville

Yountville is located on the western side of Napa, between the Mayacama Mountains to the west and the Vaca Mountains to the east. Its location midway up the valley makes its temperatures moderate by valley standards, as it still experiences some cool breezes off San Pablo Bay. The regions to the north are generally warmer and those to the south are generally cooler; however, temperatures here can drop quite a bit. While Yountville is not as famous as Rutherford, Oakville, or Stags Leap, unusually cool conditions in its vineyards sometimes produce Cabernet Sauvignon beyond comparison.

Mount Veeder

Located in the Mayacamas Mountains in central Napa, Mount Veeder is named after the volcanic peak that towers over the region. The vineyards here occupy the east-facing hillsides below the mountain range. Mount Veeder is far enough south to feel the tempering effect of maritime breezes from San Pablo Bay and receive an occasional layer of fog. Air drainage down the hillsides guards against frost, but rainfall is relatively high. The variety of soils in the region includes sandstone, light clay, volcanic ash, and shale. The two best-known varieties here are Chardonnay and Cabernet Sauvignon. The Cabernet in particular is known for its unusual varietal intensity and different structure from the average Napa Cabernet from the valley floor.

Oakville

Oakville is perhaps best known for the legendary Mondavi and Cakebread wineries, but an array of other fine wineries call the region home. Conditions vary across the region, but growing conditions are often close to perfect. In the benchland formed by six streams flowing down from the Mayacamas, the soil is gravelly and well drained. Farther east toward the Napa River, however, the soil is more alluvial with a higher content of silt and clay.

Unlike nearby Rutherford, Oakville refuses to specialize in any one variety. Instead, Oakville is known for its excellence across the board. The region's Cabernet Sauvignon is exceptional, but cool mornings and fog are perfect for Chardonnay and Sauvignon Blanc as well.

Rutherford

Rutherford is the historic heartland of Napa and one of the best-known appellations in the United States. In fact, the name is so famous that winemakers were long reluctant to give it its own AVA. The argument was that if Napa were carved up into smaller AVAs, the reputation of Napa itself might suffer as its best wines came to be associated with Rutherford instead of Napa.

The Rutherford region today is home to more than thirty wineries, many of them famous. Rutherford is slightly warmer than Oakville and not as well suited to white grapes. Cabernets made in Rutherford, on the other hand, are among the finest in Napa. Credit for these wines is usually given to the famous Rutherford Bench, an alluvial area of gravel loam left by creeks flowing down out of the Mayacamas. This soil retains moisture well, and according to some imparts local wine with a distinctive flavor known as Rutherford Dust. Whatever you call the flavor, these wines are truly exceptional.

Diamond Mountain

Home to the legendary Diamond Creek estate, the small but legendary appellation Diamond Mountain consists of a small number of vineyards scattered throughout the area. The AVA lies in the Mayacamas Range, in the far northeast of Napa Valley. Porous volcanic soil and abundant sunlight make this region ideal for vines: Yields are low, quality is high, and the Cabernet Sauvignon here is known throughout the world. In addition, the Cabernet Franc and Zinfandel are also famous, as are the Schramberg sparkling wines.

Chiles Valley

Chiles Valley is a narrow area of vines in the Vaca Mountains on the northeast edge of Napa. The maritime effects of the bay breezes do not reach this far north, but the combined effects of the 1,000-foot elevation, prevailing winds that blow throughout the valley, and air currents of the Vaca Mountains help to keep the vines cool. Nevertheless, the growing season is relatively short. The principal varieties here are Zinfandel, Cabernet Sauvignon, Chardonnay, and Sauvignon Blanc.

Howell Mountain

Howell Mountain is a large AVA on the eastern edge of Napa. The vineyards are planted on Howell Mountain, where the land is flat but high in elevation, between 1,400 and 2,200 feet. The region was well known in the nineteenth century, but the presence of the Seventh Day Adventists slowed the wine industry's recovery from Prohibition. In recent years growth has been faster, and the Howell Mountain AVA was approved in 1983.

The soil here is volcanic, and though it drains well, it is not very deep. On the main growing plateau, the soil is reddish and stony. Irrigation is common here as the land is too dry to produce much volume otherwise. The most famed variety from the region is Cabernet Sauvignon, but

Howell Mountain also produces excellent Zinfandel and Chardonnay.

CALIFORNIA'S CENTRAL COAST

Key Tastes

Pinot Noir, Syrah, Sauvignon Blanc

Central Coast Pinot Noirs and Syrahs are often called fruit bombs because of their extremely jammy, highly alcoholic, "meal in a glass" nature. Central Coast Pinots are often thick, syrupy, velvety, and sensual. Central Coast Syrah can be super rich and ripe with an attractive spiciness. Central Coast Sauvignon Blanc is often zippy, more akin to New Zealand Sauvignon Blanc than those from Napa.

If you've ever walked into a wine store and noticed that every American wine on the shelf seems to come from California, you're not imagining things. California is far and away the largest wine-producing area in North America, with more than 350,000 acres under cultivation. Production here dwarfs anything the rest of the continent can muster, and California is responsible for a staggering 90 percent of the wine produced in America.

Home to the famed regions of Napa Valley and Sonoma County, California combines innovation with Old World tradition in a unique manner specifically adapted to California's landscape. Given California's size and variety of terrain, it's understandable that California's wine production spans the entire range of varietals. The exciting aspect is that the state manages to achieve excellence in each. From the Cabernet Sauvignon in Rutherford to the Pinot Noir in Santa Barbara, California wines are known the world over.

Although there will always be a debate among purists over whether California wines can match classic Burgundy or Bordeaux, the famed Paris tasting of 1976 helped to affirm the legitimacy of the California wine industry. In the blind tasting, a panel of French judges awarded California reds and whites top honors over French varieties, thereby vindicating the production of fine wine in California and the rest of the New World. We leave it to you to do your own tests, and we hope you enjoy some fine wines along the way.

History

The oldest vineyards in California were begun by Spanish missionaries approximately 230 years ago. While viticulture quickly spread across the state, the quality of wine produced was held back by the limited potential of the grape. Originally from South America, the Mission grape was hardy but lacked the nuances of French varietals.

Despite the lack of expertise among the Spanish friars, winemaking in California continued to grow and improve. The influx of European immigrants included many with a background in viticulture, and some began to import wines from France. A growing population ensured a steady consumer base, and the gold rush of 1849 brought waves of eager prospectors. California wine continued to improve with the completion of the transcontinental railroad in 1869. However, California was not immune to the financial downturn of the 1880s or the blight of phylloxera, and 1894 saw the brief tenure of the California Wine Association, formed in order to reduce overproduction and ensure the profitability of growing grapes. Prohibition struck another blow to the industry, one from which it would not recover until the late 1960s.

Toward the end of the 1960s, the California wine industry embarked on a prolonged period of steady growth, punctuated by the results of the previously mentioned

Paris tasting. The California wine industry continues to grow and improve. Although wine consumption is down, Americans today drink higher-quality wine. Despite the instability of the industry and the sharp competition from importers, the future of Californian wine looks very bright.

Mendocino County

Located just north of Sonoma, Mendocino County's vineyards are particularly famous for the sparkling wines grown in Anderson Valley. With a diverse set of climate and soil types, however, Mendocino produces its fair share of still wines: Cabernet Sauvignon, Chardonnay, and Chenin Blanc all prosper. Redwood Valley AVA, in the northeastern corner of Mendocino's wine country, is particularly good for warm-weather varieties. Heavily forested northern Mendocino is unsuitable for viticulture, so all the major wineries, even those within Redwood Valley, are concentrated in the southern half of the county.

Mendocino County, separated from the famous Sonoma County by hilly terrain, remained isolated and relatively undeveloped well into the twentieth century. Despite a railroad connecting the capital of Mendocino to Sonoma and San Francisco, few vineyards emerged, and the enactment of Prohibition destroyed virtually all of the fledgling vineyards in the region. The region languished until the arrival of Parducci and Fetzer wineries in the 1960s. Despite their influence, the region is mostly home to dozens of small boutique wineries.

One hundred miles north of San Francisco, just above Sonoma County, the region enjoys mild winters and hot summers, the effect of high coastal ranges and the lack of maritime influences. Only one appellation within Mendocino, Anderson Valley, is affected by the coast, and it enjoys a cooler climate than the rest of the region. Most vineyards grow on the flat valleys or on low sloping hills around their borders, though a few vines are grown higher on vineyards reaching altitudes of nearly 1,600 feet. The soils here are mostly alluvial, with gravel and sandy loam very prevalent. Among the many varieties produced are Chardonnay, Chenin Blanc, Sauvignon Blanc, Cabernet Sauvignon, Carignan, and Zinfandel.

Monterey

Though historically thought to be too cool and blustery for winemaking, Monterey (which includes the Salinas Valley) has recently shown great potential. First seriously cultivated for wine in the second half of the twentieth century, Monterey winemakers struggled to find the best pairing of grape and terroir. Today, through a great deal of trial and error, the region seems to have found its niche.

The Monterey region, located along Monterey Bay, extends south down the Salinas Valley. The northern area of Monterey is a cool region that is chilled year round by the cold Pacific winds. These breezes penetrate down the Salinas Valley as well since it opens to the northwest, facing the prevailing wind. Fog is common toward the north as well, though it is generally blown off by afternoon. Cool near the coast, the dry region requires irrigation in each area, and the further inland one moves, the hotter and drier the region becomes. Vines are mostly planted on the flat plains and sloping hills along the valleys in soil that is not particularly fertile or productive. The well-draining soil is composed of silty loam, though some areas contain rock and gravel-based soil. Monterey is particularly known for its Chardonnay, Riesling, Pinot Noir, Merlot, and Pinot Blanc.

Santa Barbara County

Almost unknown thirty years ago, Santa Barbara County's wine country is rapidly becoming one of the world's premier locations for Pinot Noir. With the fabulous Santa Ynez and Santa Maria Valleys, Santa Barbara has effectively challenged France's Burgundy region, the traditional mecca of the Pinot Noir grape. The region was even featured in the recent film *Sideways*, in which two friends explore Santa Barbara's vineyards, marveling at its Pinot Noir. This film actually had a remarkable effect on California's wine market, with Pinot sales skyrocketing at the expense of other reds like Merlot.

Located south of San Luis Obispo County and north of Los Angeles, the region boasts temperatures that are uniquely suited for Pinot Noir and Chardonnay. The moderate climate allows for a long growing season without altering acidity levels and explains why the region makes such remarkable wines. Vineyards grow on south-facing, sloping hillsides and valleys. Soil is composed of sand, clay, and silt, with occasional alkaline influences. The area produces a smooth and elegant Pinot Noir, a Chardonnay that is well balanced between tropical fruit flavors and acidity, Sauvignon Blanc, and Riesling.

Santa Ynez Valley

This area of low, rolling hills and valleys represents one of California's finest, if not best, regions for Pinot Noir. As late as the 1980s, Santa Ynez Valley seemed a minor player even within the California wine scene; however, it has proved capable of producing wines rivaling even the famous Burgundies, and winemakers have pushed ahead with developing this fine wine appellation. One vineyard in particular, Sanford & Benedict, has achieved outstanding success with its smooth, elegant Pinot Noirs. Great Oaks Ranch, owned and operated by the wonderful Lippman family, produces the best Sauvignon Blanc and Syrah in the region.

Santa Maria Valley

Open to the Pacific Ocean breezes and fog to the northwest, Santa Maria Valley has a cool climate ideal for Pinot Noir and Chardonnay. Occasional spring frosts can present difficulties to winemakers, and the scarcity of rain makes irrigation a must. Though not as well known as the wines from Santa Ynez Valley, this appellation still has some great offerings of cool-weather wines.

Lake County

East of Mendocino County and northeast of Sonoma, Lake County is one of the hottest new appellations in northern California. Lake County is comprised of the Benmore Valley, Clear Lake, and Guenoc Valley AVA appellations.

Sauvignon Blanc, Chardonnay, Cabernet Sauvignon, Merlot, and Zinfandel are all prevalent, though Sauvignon Blanc is probably the best-known wine from the region.

The region's wine growing is centered around Clear Lake, a large body of water that provides a cooling effect on the otherwise hot area. The climate is further influenced by the region's high altitude—the lowest vineyards are still at 1,300 feet above sea level. Soils are a mixture of old volcanic debris and alluvial clay, and rainfall is minimal, so irrigation is required for nearly all the grapes grown in Lake County.

Sierra Foothills

Historically better known for the California gold rush than for wine, the Sierra Foothills AVA region has recently developed into a high-quality wine area. Do not be fooled by its proximity to the Central Valley of California; this hilly region is completely separate. The Sierra Foothills first came into the spotlight in the 1970s, and the region is now known for its big, bold Zinfandels, with other varieties like Sauvignon Blanc, Riesling, Barbera, Cabernet Sauvignon, and Merlot prospering as well. Grown at medium to very high altitudes, there are a variety of microclimates to fit these grapes' needs. The Sierra Foothills region contains a number of smaller subappellations named Fiddletown, El Dorado, North Yuba, and California Shenandoah Valley.

San Luis Obispo County

Encompassing the appellations of Paso Robles, Edna Valley, Arroyo Grande, and York Mountain, this relatively new wine region produces many good wines in several different microclimates. From the inland heat of Paso Robles to the cool ocean breezes of Edna Valley, with varieties from Zinfandel to Chardonnay, all prosper within San Luis Obispo County.

Located south of Monterey County and north of Santa Barbara County, the temperatures in San Luis Obispo County range from very hot inland (Paso Robles) to moderately cool in the more coastal regions like Edna Valley. Proximity to the coast also increases the amount of rain, although the region is dry overall. Vineyards grow predominantly on hillsides at altitudes of up to 1,500 feet. The higher vineyards are only grown in the York Mountain AVA, as areas like Edna Valley do not plant vineyards above six hundred feet. The soil is composed of sand, clay, and silt, with occasional alkaline influences, and many different varieties prosper here.

Central Valley

Though it produces a staggering 75 percent of California's wine, California's Central Valley makes few fine wines. The region stretches most of the length of the state, from Redding and Mount Shasta in the north to Bakersfield and the Tehachapi Mountains to the south. Two major rivers, the Sacramento and San Joaquin, drain the valley and are used extensively for irrigation. These water sources, combined with incredibly fertile soil, make California's Central Valley one of the most productive agricultural regions in the world, and vines grow incredibly well here. Fertile soils and huge harvests hurt the quality of wines produced, making Central Valley grapes worth roughly a sixth of those grown in the more coastal regions like Napa and Sonoma Counties.

Expect mostly low-quality table wines from the Central Valley. These wines are often labeled as simply red or white wine and are produced in bulk. There are a few AVAs that command a higher reputation. The appellations of Clarksburg and Lodi in particular produce superior-quality grapes to the rest of the Central Valley and should not be lumped together with the rest of its wines.

Paso Robles

Paso Robles, one of California's oldest wine production zones, has some treacherous hills. Gravity Hills, a winery owned by the Fourmeaux family, has a wine named Tumbling Tractor Zinfandel, whose name originated when their vineyard manager, Manuel, rolled his tractor all the way to the bottom of this slope while harvesting the fruit. The hills won the battle but not the war. Gravity Hills makes a delicious Killer Climb Syrah and Tumbling Tractor Zinfandel today.

OTHER FUN AVAS TO SAMPLE

Edna Valley: Cool air from the Pacific pushes into the Edna Valley keeping the climate moderate and allowing for cooler varieties of grapes to succeed in the clay and sandy loam soil.

Arroyo Grande: Southeast of Edna Valley, the Arroyo Grande has a moderate, coastal climate, making this area well suited to the production of sparkling and still wines from Chardonnay and Pinot Noir.

Santa Cruz Mountains

Though not a major wine-producing region compared to Napa and Sonoma, vines have found an interesting and unique region in the Santa Cruz Mountains. Although not an obvious choice for vineyards, many fine Chardonnays, Pinot Noirs, and a few Cabernets come from it.

The Santa Cruz Mountains occupy the space north of the town of Santa Cruz and Monterey Bay between the Santa Clara Valley and the Pacific Ocean. This is a cool and fairly wet region, though vineyards on the east side of the mountains tend to be much warmer. The Santa Cruz Mountains region is very hilly with fairly steep slopes throughout. Most vineyards are planted at the higher elevations, with vineyards in the area around Mt. Eden required to be at least 1,000 feet above sea level to avoid the coastal fog. Formed by the scraping of the oceanic crust in the former California subduction zone, the Santa Cruz Mountains consist of soft shale known as the Franciscan Formation. This stone is brittle and crumbly.

BOTTLENOTES' RECOMMENDED WINES FROM THE SANTA CRUZ MOUNTAINS

Picchetti Winery Super Tuscan 2005 (Cupertino, California)—$36.95

Thomas Fogarty Chardonnay (Santa Cruz Mountains, California)—$28.00

Atlas Peak

Created in 1992, the Atlas Peak AVA consists of a collection of vineyards growing on and around Atlas Peak Mountain. The volcanic soil drains well, though it is not particularly fertile. Of all the Sangiovese grown in California, more than a quarter comes from Atlas Peak.

Sonoma County

Sonoma County rivals Napa Valley wine production in both quantity and quality. This prolific region lies to the west of Napa and runs along the coastal range until it hits San Francisco Bay to the south. With an extremely varied climate, and countless different soil types, Sonoma County makes wines of all kinds, from delicate and elegant Pinot Noir and lush Chardonnay in the cooler zones of Los Carneros and Green Valley to bold Zinfandel and Cabernet in the hot Alexander Valley. Sonoma County is also a major tourist destination for San Francisco Bay Area locals and visitors from around the world. Its smaller, more rustic vineyards provide a welcome contrast to the quasi-châteaux of neighboring Napa Valley.

From the 1940s through 1960, winemaking in Sonoma was dominated by overproduction and governmental regulations; however, the wine boom of the 1960s led to the explosion of vineyards and wineries that exists in the county to this day. Behind the famous Napa Valley, Sonoma County represents the second-most valuable and prestigious wine zone in California.

Located west of the Napa and Central Valleys, Sonoma County stretches north from San Francisco Bay up along the Russian River. Sonoma County's climate varies extensively according to location within its borders. Southern vineyards around Petaluma and San Francisco Bay receive cool bay breezes and fog year round, while vineyards further north bask in hot summers and experience cooler winters than their southern counterparts. Vines grow on moderate slopes and on the flat river and creek valley floors. Some steeper slopes have recently been planted as well. The soil of Sonoma County varies greatly. A remnant of the former California subduction zone, much of the region's soil was scraped off the top of the oceanic plate as it slid under the North American continent. Sonoma Valley consists of low-fertility loams, while the Russian River Valley has very fertile alluvial soil. The Dry Creek area's soil is gravelly, with some volcanic soil.

SONOMA SPECIALTIES

Chalk Hill: The whitish color of the earth in Chalk Hill is due to ancient volcanic ash deposits spewed by nearby Mount St. Helena and mainly produces Chardonnay.

Sonoma Mountains: Has an ideal terroir for the production of Merlot and Sauvignon Blance.

Sonoma Valley: Excellent Cabernet Sauvignon and Zinfandel to the north and Pinot Noir and Chardonnay to the south.

Northern Sonoma: Encompasses the north and east areas of Sonoma County, including the appellations of Alexander Valley, Dry Creek Valley, Russian River Valley, Chalk Hill, and Knights Valley.

Dry Creek Valley: Everything from floral whites like Sauvignon Blanc, which takes on an herbaceous quality in Dry Creek, to the bold red Zinfandel. Grassy, bell pepper–flavored Cabernet Sauvignon and Merlot and Chardonnay also grow here.

Russian River Valley: Cooler than many of its neighbors, Pinot Noir, Pinot Gris, and Chardonnay prosper here.

Alexander Valley: Perfectly suited for Cabernet Sauvignon and Merlot (though Chardonnay, Nebbiolo, and Sangiovese are also grown).

Sonoma County Green Valley AVA: Sandy, loamy soil combined with the cool climate make Sonoma County Green Valley an excellent location for sparkling wine and Pinot Noir vineyards.

Sonoma Coast: Encompasses all the appellations within the cooler western side of Sonoma County and the area near San Francisco Bay.

Knights Valley: Well suited for the Cabernet Sauvignon variety, though other grapes are grown here as well.

Los Carneros: Straddling both Napa and Sonoma Counties, the cooler climate of this AVA best suits Pinot Noir and Chardonnay, though a number of other varieties are produced here as well.

CHILE

Key Tastes

> Carmenére, Syrah, Sauvignon Blanc, Pinot Noir

Chilean terroir is truly distinct. Carmenére, similar to Merlot, is a low-yielding grape that is rarely grown outside of Chile. Syrah from Chile creates bold, peppery wines. Sauvignon Blanc from Chile has piercing aromas and crisp acidity. Pinot Noir from Chile offers notes of berries, low tannin, and medium acidity. Bottlenotes' favorite Chilean wines come from Kingston Family Vineyards in the Casablanca Valley.

Extending nearly four hundred fifty years, Chile's involvement with wine began with the arrival of the Spanish Conquistadors. These soldiers and explorers brought vine seeds with them from Europe, promptly introducing these species to the Americas.

History

The first vineyard in Chile, established in 1540 by Spaniard Francisco de Aguirre, adapted well in the northern town of La Serena. This success led to further plantings around the central Santiago area. At this time the chief grape was País, which grows easily but has weak flavors.

The fledgling Chilean wine industry came under attack from both sides: Neither the indigenous peoples nor the Spanish winemakers supported its efforts. The Spanish settlements were attacked and the vineyards destroyed, and what little wine was produced could not be sold outside of the country.

After independence in 1822, the wine industry began to improve. A wine and agricultural school was established, and French and Italian immigrants began to improve and expand Chile's vineyards. During the phylloxera epidemic of the late nineteenth and early twentieth centuries, Chile's geographical isolation kept its vines safe, and its wine exports filled much of the demand in Europe and North America.

In the 1930s, overseas demand reduced as European wineries began to recover. Furthermore, the events of World War II cut shipping lines and isolated Chile even more. Overproduction became so rampant that laws were put in place to stem the disastrous trend. In the 1980s, Chile finally began to emerge from its viticultural woes, investing heavily in technology and modernization techniques to improve its vineyards. These efforts paid off handsomely with the rise of democracy in the 1990s. In the last ten years of the twentieth century, Chile's revenue from wine exports increased dramatically, and vine cultivation expanded throughout the country's wine regions.

Today Chile leads its rival South American wine-producing countries both in terms of volume and quality of its exports. Cheap land and labor costs keep wine prices low, so the country's wines have been particularly successful in the cheaper wine market.

Valle del Maipó (Maipó Valley)

Situated just south of Santiago within the Central Valley, the Maipó Valley has warm weather cooled by the Andes and is a popular destination for wine tourists. The valley contains many of Chile's oldest wineries: Concha y Toro, Santa Rita, and Cousiño Macul. Maipó is best known for its Cabernet Sauvignon.

The first vineyards were planted along the Maipó River in the sixteenth century, making this one of the oldest wine-growing areas in South America. Maipó's wine production increased quickly due to its proximity to Santiago and remained successful throughout Chile's wine struggles in the first half of the twentieth century. Recently, Santiago's suburban sprawl has begun to encroach upon the vineyards of Maipó, so vineyards are now being planted farther to the south and west, away from the city and on the flat valley floor. Soil in the Maipó Valley is rocky, with broad alluvial sands and volcanic materials, and produces Cabernet Sauvignon, Merlot, Chardonnay, and Sauvignon Blanc.

Valle de Curicó (Curicó Valley)

One hundred and twenty miles south of Santiago, the Curicó Valley is an expansive region with plenty of space for wine production. Blessed with a true Mediterranean climate of warm summers and cool winters, this subregion produces good red and white varieties of wine, although a lot of basic wine is made as well. With its rolling hills, microclimates ideal for fine wines are abundant, and local wineries have taken advantage. Even foreign wine companies, such as Spain's Miguel Torres, have invested in the Curicó Valley area. Red wines dominate the region, with much of the land devoted to growing the low-quality Pais variety.

CHECK OUT CHILE

Atacama and Coquimbo: hot, desert regions; most grapes are either still used to sell as grapes or to produce Pisco, a light-colored brandy

Valle del Elqui: mainly produces Pisco

Aconcagua: dry climate moderated by coastal influences, making this one of Chile's top wine regions

Valle de Aconcagua (Aconcagua Valley): fruity Merlot, a strong and fruity Syrah, and an intense, fruity Cabernet Sauvignon

Valle de Casablanca (Casablanca Valley): exciting, high-quality white wines, like a classy, fruity Chardonnay and a fantastic Sauvignon Blanc; also produces an elegant and smooth Pinot Noir

Valle Central (Central Valley): broad spectrum of wine—and produces lots of it! Best varieties here are reds.

Valle de Rapel (Rapel Valley): Try their Carmenere, which does well in this cool climate.

Valle de Maule (Maule Valley): Reds make a strong showing, but whites are the dominant grape produced—particularly Chardonnay and Sauvignon Blanc, as well as Pais.

Southern Region: separated into two subregions, Itata and Bío-Bío, and both produce Gewürztraminer, Pinot Noir, and Chardonnay—though the better quality wine will likely come from Bio-Bio

ARGENTINA

Key Tastes

Malbec, Torrontes, Cabernet Sauvignon, Merlot

Malbec has become Argentina's most iconic red wine grape variety, and the country produces a rich, dark wine with hints of leather, chocolate, and dark berry. Torrontes claims the throne as the most iconic white wine grape variety from Argentina; it has been compared to Viognier with its fruity aromas of peach, flowers, and oranges.

Although the first European grapes were introduced from Chile in 1556, winemaking grew slowly over the next two hundred and fifty years. Independence from Spain in 1816 proved a watershed event for Argentina's wine industry as a wave of new immigrants from winemaking countries in Europe provided a thirsty domestic market and the expertise to begin low domestic production. Many of these new residents hailed from Italy and Spain and lent their countries' influence to local grape varieties.

History

In the mid-nineteenth century, Argentina imported grapes of the classic French varieties for the first time, and an academy of agriculture in Mendoza trained students in the French school of winemaking. New irrigation began to cover the naturally dry land, and viticulture expanded across the country. With so many trends in its favor, Argentina successfully exported wine around the world until the 1920s.

The global depression of the interwar years hurt exports, and the 1920s marked the beginning of years of economic and political instability. For fifty years there was little foreign investment in wine technology and quality suffered. All this time, however, the domestic market remained strong and Argentina became known as a mass producer of mediocre wine.

Unfortunately, the situation would get worse before it got better. During the 1970s, wine consumption in Argentina began a sharp decline, and the 1980s saw severe overproduction that ran many of the lower-quality vineyards out of business. While Chile reduced yields in the 1990s and improved quality, Argentina actually increased yields in spite of overproduction. While there is little precipitation, irrigation is quite cheap, allowing farmers to leave the faucet running and watch yields go up. Quality, of course, disappears in this method of farming.

Only a few winemakers were determined enough to resist that temptation, but they soon gave the world a taste of Argentina's potential. As other winemakers realized how much profit and honor could be won from the international market, they began to start planting in higher densities and growing for quality rather than volume. This experience is starting to pay dividends, and Argentinian wine is steadily improving. The coming decade will prove crucial to the future of Argentinian wine—truly a country to watch.

Today Argentina is a country of possibility. Argentina is the world's fifth-largest wine producer, after France, Italy, Spain, and the United States, but the vast majority of its grapes produce mediocre-quality bulk wine. The future of its winemaking industry lies in exports, not in bulk, but the country currently exports only 7 percent of its product.

Mendoza

If you've ever tasted a wine in Argentina, chances are it was made in Mendoza. At 58,000 square miles, Mendoza contains approximately 75 percent of the vines in the country, and Malbec, Cabernet Sauvignon, and Torrontes are the grapes of choice.

Located more than six hundred miles west of Buenos Aires, the Mendoza region is enormous and includes a wide variety of soils and microclimates. Mendoza is so large that it is broken into several subregions, including Luján de Cuyo, San Rafael, and Tupungato. There is considerable variation throughout Mendoza, but the soil is generally dry and desertlike. The modern winemaking industry here owes its existence to irrigation. The high slopes of Mendoza are home to the country's signature Torrontes, and all three varieties are grown here. Torrontes Riojano is the most common, but Torrontes Sanjuanino and Torrontes Mendocino are widespread as well. These wines are known for their light-body, crisp feel in the mouth, and their aromas reminiscent of a fragrant Muscat or Gewürztraminer.

AMAZING ARGENTINA

Rio Negro: ideal for Sauvignon Blanc and Chardonnay, and Pinot Noir

La Rioja: oxidation remains a major problem here, and the region is best known for its Malbec

Salta: produces Torrontes that thrives on the cool mountain terroir, which captures its fruity flavors

San Juan: keep an eye on the Syrah from this region; it might give you a pleasant surprise sometime soon

PORTUGAL

Key Tastes

Fortified wines: Port, Madeira

Like Spain, Portugal traces the origins of its wine production to the Phoenicians (1100 b.c.), Carthaginians (250 b.c.), and Romans (100 b.c.). Portugal also underwent periods of Visigoth and Moor control before Christians drove them from most of the Iberian Peninsula at the end of the thirteenth century. Despite the changing imperial powers, viticulture continued to exist, albeit at a low rate, until the Christians had driven the Moors out of the country.

For hundreds of years, Portugal has enjoyed international fame for its Port wines and its Madeira. Today some of its red table wines are becoming increasingly known, often made from the red grape variety Tourgia Nacional.

History

Early in its exporting days, Portugal brought wine to England in exchange for food and goods. To ensure that Portugal's big, tannic red wines survived the passage to England, merchants often fortified the wine with brandy before the voyage. According to legend, a lone enterprising English merchant decided to fortify the wine during, rather than after, the fermentation. The brandy added sweetness to the fermenting wine, and Port was born.

However, Portugal's greatest contribution to the wine industry may have been when English shippers discovered that stoppers made from the bark of cork could preserve a wine for a long ocean voyage. While the English may have made the discovery, most of the world's cork trees grow in Spain and Portugal. To this day, Portugal is still the world's leading producer of cork.

Unfortunately, the end of the nineteenth century marked the beginning of a difficult time for Portugal. The vineyards were hit especially hard by the phylloxera blight, and political disruptions in the twentieth century made recovery difficult. A bright spot came in 1916 when the world community agreed that only Portugal could legally call its wine Port and Madeira, but quality in the highly collectivized system remained generally low. Only when Portugal was admitted to the E.U. in 1986 did winemaking begin to improve rapidly. Today the Portuguese wine industry concentrates on making quality wine and improving its reputation in the international market.

The Port Region

The Port trade is at the center of Portugal's winemaking industry, and by international agreement no country except Portugal is allowed to label its wines as Port. In Port, distilled brandy is added to the wine, arresting fermentation and leaving behind a touch of sweetness and residual sugar. The result is a world-famous dessert wine of 19 to 20 percent alcohol.

Douro

Also known as the Upper Douro and Porto e Douro, this region is responsible for the production of Portugal's famed Port wines. The soil here is mostly schist, a bed of rock and mineral. Although roots must struggle to reach the wetter earth beneath the hard schist, viticulture has flourished here for hundreds of years.

Today the Douro region is beginning to produce some excellent red wines, known for the spicy flavor and full body that they share with Port. It remains best known, however, for the Port that made it famous. Although Port is aged in traditional caves in the coastal city of Oporto, it is grown and produced in the Douro.

The Douro Valley is located along the Douro River as it flows out of Spain in northeast Portugal. Summers are dry and hot; winters are mild and wet. As you move northeast away from the Atlantic, the climate becomes more continental. The valley is hilly throughout, with slopes sometimes reaching very steep angles. The best Port varieties are thought to be Touriga Nacional, Tinta Cão, Tinto Roriz, Tinta Barroca, Touriga Francesa, and Tinta Amarela.

Alentejo

Alentejo is a vast agricultural region in southern Portugal that is known not for its wine but rather for its endless grain farms and forests of cork trees. More than half of the cork produced in Portugal comes from this region.

Growing grapes here is difficult due to the region's harsh climate. Rainfall is scarce, and summer temperatures can be brutal. Modern technology makes it easier to overcome these obstacles, and most Alentejo reds contain Aragonêz, Periquita, and Trincadeira Preta. From the Aragonêz and the Periquita, the wines obtain their blackberry and licorice flavors; from the Trincadeira Preta, they receive their structure. These wines are perfect companions to roasted meats and strong cheeses traditional in Portuguese cuisine.

Bairrada

The hardy Baga occupies the majority of the region's fertile clay vineyards. All Bairrada wine, in fact, must be

50 percent Baga. The Baga grape produces stout, dark, and tannic wine with a distinctive taste.

Setúbal

Located south of Lisbon, the Setúbal Peninsula lies between the Sado and Tagus Rivers. The rivers form estuaries here and moderate the climate, creating stable, warm temperatures and dependable rainfall. The most famous wine here is Moscatel do Setúbal, a sweet fortified wine made primarily from the Muscat grape, which is golden and redolent with caramel, honey, walnuts, spice, and apricot.

Vinho Verde

Literally "green wine," but the phrase refers to the fact that it is meant to be drunk young, not the wine's color. Vinho Verde is known for its bright, very dry, semi-sparkling white (often Alvarinho), although fully half the production here is red.

Dão

Located to the east of Bairrada, Dão is known for its excellent red table wines. The region is surrounded by granite-rich hills that shield it from the influence of the Atlantic, and the slopes are often so steep that vineyards must be planted in terraces.

Madeira

Located off the coast of Morocco, Madeira is actually closer to Africa than to Spain. Madeira is known for its plentiful sunshine and rainfall, its rich clay and volcanic soil, and its gorgeous terraced hillsides.

The four varieties of Madeira are Sercial, Verdelho, Bual, and Malmsey. Sercial is the driest and lightest of the group, followed by Verdelho. Both have naturally high acidity and are often served as apéritifs. Bual is sweeter and is often served with coffee or caramel desserts.

The sweetest is Malmsey, made from exceptionally ripe grapes. The sugar in this famous wine is so high that these wines can age well for one hundred years, but its high acidity ensures it never tastes too sweet.

SPAIN

Key Tastes

Tempranillo, Albariño

Tempranillo, whether blended or not, forms the backbone of wines throughout Spain but is at its best in Rioja and the Navarra. Its white wine complement, Albariño, is a white wine grape native to Spain that offers bright acidity and aromas of ripe nectarines.

The Phoenicians, who settled around present-day Cádiz around 1100 B.C., were most likely the first producers of Spanish wine. Over a thousand years later, the Carthaginians and Romans simultaneously invaded different parts of Spain around 200 B.C., and both promptly expanded viticulture into their new territories. The Romans eventually gained control of all the Carthaginian holdings, and wine production and export in all of the Roman Empire continued to grow.

History

Winemaking continued, albeit at a slower rate of growth, throughout the collapse of the Roman Empire and subsequent domination by the Visigoths; however, the Moorish invasion in A.D. 711 dealt a serious blow to viticulture. Although not all Moors abstained from wine, their religion prohibited its consumption, resulting in a sharp reduction in the number of wine consumers. Only the significant Jewish and Christian population within the Moorish Empire kept the wine industry alive during the six hundred years of Muslim rule.

Northern Spain remained Christian, and Navarra, Aragon, Castilla y León, and Barcelona worked together to defeat the Moors to the south and create a Christian Spain. In 1492, Spain was officially reunited under Ferdinand and Isabella, and the wine industry flourished. This brief expansion was quickly curbed by the effects of the war between Spain and England, ending with the defeat of the Spanish Armada.

Spanish wine production expanded slowly from the sixteenth to the nineteenth century but was devastated by the phylloxera epidemic of the late nineteenth century. Fortunately, French immigrants replanted the vineyards with superior grapes, and the region was temporarily restored. In the twentieth century, Spanish winemaking ground to yet another halt as political pressures led to the Spanish Civil War, after which nationalist dictator Francisco Franco isolated Spain to such a degree that Spanish wine stayed within its borders. Only in 1975, after Franco's death, did Spain truly recover and blossom into the important wine producer it is today.

Suffering from a reputation as a producer of lowly bulk wine, Spain had nearly been written off the map as a legitimate wine-producing country. However, with the death of Franco and the birth of a modern government, Spain's fortunes quickly reversed. Today Spain is known for quality wines of many varieties from nearly every major region of the country, including fabulous Tempranillo-based wines from Rioja and Navarra, sparkling Cava from Penedès, the famous Sherry from the Jerez district to the south, and luscious white Albariño-based wines from the northwest corner of Galicia. With a solid organizational system and a determined effort from winemakers, Spain's wine is poised for international fame.

Jerez (Sherry)

Located in southern Spain near the Strait of Gibraltar, Jerez is uniquely suited to the production of Sherry. It is comparable to France's Champagne region in that it has a virtual monopoly on Sherry based upon natural geologic and climatic forces. Other areas in the world have attempted to produce Sherry, but none can match the attributes of the original region. The soil and hot, dry winds combine to create the ideal situation for its production. Moreover, in recent years, the tightening of E.U. geographical indications laws has strengthened Jerez's legal status as the sole producer of the actual Sherry wine.

Two different winds play a key role in Sherry's production: the wet Poniente wind from the Atlantic, which allows for the growth of the flor yeast in Sherry Fino; and the dry Levante, which heats and dries the grapes on the vines well into their ripening stage, drastically altering the metabolism process of Sherry grapes. Vineyards grow everywhere, from the flat coastal plains to the hilly terrain farther inland all the way to the high plateau of Málaga at over 1,600 feet above sea level. The soil in Jerez is crucial to its wine. Called Albariza, it's white in color and incredibly rich in lime. The soil soaks up rain during the brief wet season and then forms a tight shell on the surface, insulating the water from evaporation. Additionally, its sparkling color reflects the sunlight onto the grapes as they ripen. The region produces the varieties Palomino, Pedro Ximénez, and Moscatel.

Rioja and Navarra

Rioja and Navarra comprise the finest wine production area in Spain. While Rioja's products have been criticized for an excess of oak, the vanilla-oak flavor is the defining characteristic of a Rioja wine.

Though Navarra's wines aren't quite the same caliber as those from Rioja, they have been marketed successfully in their own lower-price category. Known for rosés, Navarra improved its production of Tempranillo as well.

The major wine districts within these two regions are the Rioja Alta, Rioja Alavesa, Rioja Baja, Baja Montaña, Ribera Alta, Ribera Baja, Tierra Estella, and Valdizarbe. Of these districts, the first three Rioja names are the most well known.

Located just south of Bilbao, Rioja and Navarra lie between the Pyrenees to the northeast and the Sierra de la Demanda to the southwest. The surrounding mountains keep the regions fairly warm and protect it from powerful winds and other negative maritime influences. Winters can be cold and often foggy, while summers are moderately warm. Vineyards grow in the hills in and around Rioja, with a few spilling down into the valleys. Soil in Rioja and Navarra is heavily influenced by limestone, with pockets of sandstone and clay. The region produces Tempranillo, Viura, and Garnacha. Most red Rioja wines are a blend of roughly 70 percent Tempranillo, 15 percent Garnacha, and the remaining 15 percent divided evenly between Graciano and Mazuelo. White Riojas are 95 percent Viura and 5 percent Malvasía.

Penedès

Located near Barcelona in the Spanish state of Catalonia, Penedès is the home of Cava, Spain's well-known traditional sparkling wine. In fact, outside of Champagne, Cava is the most famous sparkling wine name in the world. Two major companies, Codorníu and Freixenet, produce the majority of Cava using the Parellada, Macabéo, and Xarel-lo grapes, and experimentation with other varieties remains controversial.

The climate is distinctly Mediterranean near the coast, becoming more continental in the Terra Alta zone. The coastal area must cope with frequent fogs, while the inland area suffers from occasional frosts and hot summers. Vineyards grow on flat plains and hills alike, the highest vines being found at 1,300 feet of elevation. Soil varies extensively across the region, including granite, limestone, clay, and alluvial sand. Varieties produced here include Viura (Macabéo), Xarel-lo, Parellada, Cabernet Sauvignon, Garnacha, Mourvèdre, Samsó, and Tempranillo.

SPANISH SECRETS

La Mancha: largely bulk wine, though recently there has been an increase of fine-wine production

Ribera del Duero: a promising region that looks to rival the great Rioja

Galicia: Rías Baixas and Ribeiro: famous for wines made from Albariño, Torrontés, and Treixadura grapes

FRANCE

Key Tastes (by region)

Burgundy:	Chardonnay, Pinot Noir
Bordeaux blends:	Cabernet Sauvignon, Merlot, Cabernet Franc, Malbec, Petit Verdot
Rhône:	Syrah, Grenache, Mouvedre
Provence:	rosés, Mouvedre
Loire:	Cabernet Franc, Carignan, Gamay, Cinsault

Burgundian Chardonnay is full-flavored, easy drinking, and hardly ever sharp or aggressive. Burgundian Pinot Noir is elegant and subtle.

Bordeaux Cabernet Sauvignon often has high levels of phenolic compounds, leading to good tannin and structure. Bordeaux Merlot has a soft, lush, fruity character.

Bordeaux Cabernet Franc is mainly used for its bright fruitiness and is a lighter, less tannic version of Cabernet Sauvignon, with a green-peppery, leafy character. Bordeaux Malbec, considered a lesser variety in France, adds body to blends. Bordeaux Petit Verdot is used in Bordeaux blends to add acidity to the wine.

In the northern Rhône, Syrah produces a dense, smoky, more herbal wine packed with black pepper and berry flavors. Rhône Grenache is complex and earthy, with ripe, spicy fruit, and distinct aromas of white pepper. Rhône Mouvedre is a luscious grape with expressive notes of berry.

Provence Mouvedre is a luscious grape with expressive notes of berry.

Loire Cabernet Franc is mainly used for its bright fruitiness. Loire Carignan is a harsher, full-bodied red grape that is used to support the structure and density of blends. Loire's easy-drinking Gamay is fruitful and best drunk within a few years of bottling. Loire Cinsault, with its subtle blue fruit, spice, and nuts, is particularly popular in the creation of rosé.

France, with the greatest abundance of the highest-quality wine in the world, is the measure by which all other countries are judged. Aided by its ideal geography and diverse climates, France contains classic winemaking regions that consistently produce exquisite wines. Each region produces specific grape varieties, carefully selected by experimentation over the course of several hundred years. The AOC (Appellation d'Origin Contrôlée) carefully manages this system, which has become the standard for wine law worldwide. Within France lies an incredible amount of variety, from classic Bordeaux to Alsatian Riesling. The multitudes of wines are categorized by region, rather than variety, but all share complexity and quality. Elegant French wine is truly the pinnacle of viticulture.

History

The growth of French viticulture shares the origins of all European winemaking. First begun by the Greeks in the sixth century B.C., it was expanded and organized by the Romans. The church, as in Italy, protected the vineyards after the fall of Rome, particularly since many vineyards bordered monasteries, and their products were used in religious rituals. Over time, a strong traditional system emerged in the Middle Ages, which continued until the rise of Napoleon in the nineteenth century.

Historically, French law followed primogeniture, the system in which the oldest son inherited the entirety of his father's wealth. Under Napoleon, the abolishment of aristocracy included the end of primogeniture, requiring each estate to be split equally amongst all children. While perhaps more fair, Napoleon's system wreaked havoc on wine-producing estates. Under primogeniture, a wine estate could pass from father to son for generations with little change, allowing specific traditions to develop, molded to each individual estate. Napoleon's law led to fragmentation, splitting single vineyards among as many as ten owners. These laws have made France's land system somewhat bewildering to outsiders and are the reason Burgundy today is such a labyrinthine patchwork of small owners and vineyards.

In the late nineteenth century, the phylloxera aphid from North America began destroying France's vines. The wine industry was only saved by grafting the classic French varieties onto phylloxera-resistant American rootstock.

Prices followed the upward trajectory of French wines' fame and prestige, particularly those of certain well-known regions and producers. Seeing the rich potential for fraud, the French government began to safeguard these reputations to protect both the growers and the consumers.

Alsace

Resting between the Vosges Mountains and the Rhine River, Alsace has incorporated French and German styles of winemaking into its own unique tradition. Although disputed over by France and Germany for more than one thousand years, the last switch occurring after World War I, little appears to have changed for generations: The region boasts ruined castles, stone churches, and old villages. The famous white wine is made from German varieties in the French style. Americans often think of German varieties (and by extension those from Alsace) as overly sweet; however, this is not the case.

The Alps lend variety to Alsace's soil; consequently, the region produces an abundant amount of varieties, including Riesling, Gewürztraminer, Pinot Gris, Pinot Noir, Muscat, Pinot Blanc, Chasselas, and Sylvaner. Chasselas and Sylvaner are blending grapes that are losing acreage to the more noble Riesling, while the others can stand alone.

The most popular variety in Alsace, Riesling is bone dry, with steely acidity and floral aromas that mature into flint and wet slate. Gewürztraminer, Alsace's second signature wine, is fruit-forward with high acidity, making it ideally suited for drinking with spicy food. Also in Alsace's repertoire is the often-underrated Pinot Gris, which combines the spice of Gewürztraminer with the acidity of the Riesling.

Other varieties include Pinot Blanc, a simple white wine with a clean acidity and a crisp dryness, and even a little Pinot Noir, which in Alsace is light and soft with strawberry flavors. Sparkling wine in the region is called Crémant d'Alsace and consists of Pinot Blanc and possibly Riesling. Crémant d'Alsace is growing in popularity and currently represents about 10 percent of all wine made in Alsace.

The final major Alsatian wine is the deep and rich Vendage Terdive. Literally "late picked," Vendage Terdive hangs longer on the vine, developing additional sugars to create a semisweet wine with increased amounts of alcohol. Only Riesling, Gewürztraminer, Muscat, and Pinot Gris are acceptable varieties, additional sugars may not be added, and the grapes need not be botrytized. Vendage Terdive can possess flavors of wonderful richness and depth.

Champagne

Located roughly ninety miles northeast of Paris, near the Ardennes Forest and Belgium, cold and wet Champagne has quite variable weather, which makes spring and fall difficult for winemakers. The nearby Atlantic keeps the summers cool. Vineyards grow on the gentle hills of the region, typically facing south to maximize warmth and sunlight. The soil of Champagne consists of a chalky limestone, which drains well but allows for some water retention. The limestone-based soil creates grapes with high acidity, which is essential to the production of Champagne's sparkling wines. The important (and only!) varieties are Chardonnay, Pinot Meunier, and Pinot Noir.

Languedoc

Languedoc-Roussillon, which mainly produces red wine, also has the distinction of being France's largest producer of wine. Though robust and powerful, these wines generally cannot compare with a good Burgundy or Bordeaux; however, they are priced accordingly.

Located in southern France, west of the Rhône, Languedoc hugs the Mediterranean and stretches across vast open fields and hillsides from Nîmes to the Spanish border. Although it traditionally grows varieties typical to the South of France, such as Carignan, Cinsault, and Grenache, Languedoc has recently begun producing more Syrah, Cabernet Sauvignon, and Merlot.

Viticulture in Languedoc differs from the rest of France as grapes are mechanically harvested in the manner of corn or wheat. This low-cost technique has cemented Languedoc's reputation as France's bargain basement.

But that is not to say that Languedoc doesn't make some excellent wines. The region owes a great deal to Australian company BRL Hardy, which purchased the Domaine de la Baume vineyard in 1990 and produced some stunning wines that showed the world Languedoc's potential. In particular, BRL Hardy implemented the idea that a great Languedoc is better than a decent Bordeaux, particularly in terms of cost. Recently purchased by a French company, Domaine de la Baume has continued in the same vein.

Bordeaux

Arguably France's most famous winemaking region, Bordeaux produces approximately a quarter of the country's wine. Blended red wines from the region—a combination of a specific set of varietals—are distinctive enough that they are simply known as "Bordeaux." Like Burgundy, Bordeaux is inseparable from the face of the French wine industry, providing a standard against which all other wines are judged.

Unsurprisingly, these wines can fetch the highest prices in the world, and have done so for several hundred years. The French system actually categorizes the châteaux by price, and has done so since Napoleon III's classification of 1855. The classification, conducted by the Bordeaux Chamber of Commerce, rated the wines based upon their prices and separated the sixty-one most expensive reds into five crus, or growths.

At the time, four wines were classified as premiers crus, or first growths: Château Lafite Rothschild and Château Latour (from Pauillac), Château Margaux (Margaux), and Château Haut-Brion (Pessac-Léognan). Only one change has been made to the original classification: In 1973, after nearly fifty years of lobbying, the Baron Philippe de Rothschild convinced the French Minister of Agriculture to elevate the status of Pauillac's Château Mouton Rothschild to premier cru status.

Bordeaux is situated in the Gironde *département* on the coast of southwest France where two rivers—the Garonne and the Dordogne—meet to the north of the town of Bordeaux. Together they form an estuary called the Gironde River that continues out to the Atlantic Ocean. The city of Bordeaux's location at the mouth of the Garonne has been a major contribution to the commercial success of the region's wine production.

These rivers divide the region into three main districts: the right bank, the left bank, and entre-deux-mers ("between two seas"). Bordeaux also lies between the brandy producing regions of Cognac to the north and Armagnac to the south.

Bordeaux enjoys a mild, maritime climate that is moderated by the Atlantic Ocean and the Gironde River. The left bank appellations of the Médoc are the most protected by these bodies of water. In addition to this natural heat regulator, the Médoc is protected from ocean winds by a strip of pine forests that runs up the coast. Farther to the southeast, in Graves and Sauternes, the temperatures are a bit warmer and humidity tends to be high. The humidity brings both the unfortunate potential for frost and the ideal conditions for the formation of noble rot. Morning mists from tributaries of the Garonne River along with sunny afternoons are important contributors to the overall clime. On the right bank, temperatures are lower, and the overall climate is more continental. These areas also have higher rainfall and are less protected from ocean winds. The entre-deux-mers appellations also receive more rainfall and winds than the Médoc.

The soil composition varies greatly throughout Bordeaux and governs which type of grapes to plant. Bordeaux almost exclusively produces blends, and the character of a given wine reflects the varieties used in addition to terroir. Sauvignon Blanc and Sémillon are the main white grapes, while Muscadelle is used mainly to impart floral and fruity flavors to white blends. For red grapes, Merlot and Cabernet Franc are widely planted in Saint-Émilion and Pomerol, while Cabernet Sauvignon is more common in the Médoc and Graves. A typical Bordeaux white is crisp and dry with herbal aromas. A typical red is composed of Merlot, Cabernet Sauvignon, and Cabernet Franc and is full-bodied and complex, with heavy tannins and aromas of cedar, coffee, and blackberry.

Haut-Médoc

This area comprises slightly more than the southern half of the Médoc Peninsula, which spans the distance between the city of Bordeaux and the Atlantic Ocean. The appellation enjoys a mild climate, as a thick forest that runs along the Atlantic coast moderates the maritime influences. These trees disperse the detrimental cold ocean breezes that would otherwise reach the vineyards. Although summers are warm, the unpredictable rain can make vintages vary extensively in quality. While the majority of Bordeaux is flat, the Haut-Médoc contains some gentle hillsides facing the river. One reason for the Haut-Médoc's superior quality is its well drained, gravely soils. Cabernet Sauvignon excels here and is the main variety in most blends.

The Haut-Médoc region produces many of Bordeaux's best wines, and arguably the finest wines in the world. Only red wines from the region are allowed to carry the appellation on their label, while white wines are simply labeled "Bordeaux." Within the Haut-Médoc are the six famous communal appellations of Saint-Éstephe, Pauillac, Saint-Julien, Listrac, Moulis, and Margaux.

PLACES IN THE HAUT-MÉDOC

Saint-Éstephe: A left bank commune that produces wines made from Cabernet Sauvignon, Merlot, Cabernet

Franc, Petit Verdot, and Malbec. The most famous château among the estates of Saint-Éstephe is Château Cos d'Estournel.

Pauillac: South of Saint-Éstephe, Pauillac contains three of the great premiers crus on the left bank of Bordeaux: Château Latour, Château Lafite Rothschild, and Château Mouton Rothschild.

Saint-Julien: Softer and suppler than those made in Pauillac, these are bigger than the wines in the more southern area of Margaux.

Margaux: Often characterized as feminine, soft, and supple, premier cru Château Margaux has been considered the best wine in the world.

Listrac and Moulis: While these appellations also produce some excellent wines, they lack the power and finesse of their more famous competitors.

Sauternes and Barsac

Sauternes and Barsac are arguably the world's best appellations for sweet wine. Lush and complex, they are made primarily from Sémillon with smaller amounts of Sauvignon Blanc and Muscadelle. This region has ideal conditions for the formation of noble rot, also known as *Botrytis cinerea*. The combination of humid, misty mornings and sunny afternoons are perfect for the breeding of an indigenous strain of *Botrytis cinerea*. This noble rot shrivels the grapes and concentrates flavors, which results in an amazingly well structured golden and sweet wine. Although many other wines are made using grapes affected by botrytis, Sauternes is unique in the relatively high level of acidity that balances out the sugar in the wine.

Geographically within Graves, Sauternes and Barsac lie near the confluence of the Ciron and Garonne Rivers. The vineyards lie along the small Ciron River, and when the cold water of Ciron mixes with the warmth of the major Garonne River, a mist is formed that lies over the appellations. Consequently, this humid air creates an ideal situation for the formation of the botrytized wine.

Fairly hilly, Sauternes and Barsac have soil that is generally sandy and gravelly, with subsoils of clay and occasional limestone. Important varieties include Sauvignon Blanc, Sémillon, and Muscadelle. The dessert wines tend to be incredibly sweet, with flavors of fig, lemon, honey, and apricots.

Graves

As with Bordeaux, Graves is characterized by its delicious red wines. Smoother and fruitier than Bordeaux, blends contain a larger proportion of Merlot. Graves also produces high-quality whites from Sauvignon Blanc and Sémillon. While the Médoc appellations are pure red wine regions, whites from Graves are of top quality and bear its name on their labels.

The best wines, both red and white, are produced in a subappellation called Pessac-Léognan. One château in particular, Château Haut-Brion, was classified as a premier cru in 1855. Haut-Brion has been owned by Americans since 1935 and consistently produces stellar reds from Cabernet Sauvignon, Merlot, and Cabernet Franc and a delicious white wine blend of Sémillon and Sauvignon Blanc.

The boundaries of Graves begin at the outskirts of Bordeaux and stretch over thirty miles to the south on the left bank of the Garonne River. Very similar to the Haut-Médoc, the climate of this appellation is mild year round, with maritime influences moderated by a thick forest along the Atlantic coast. These trees serve to disperse detrimental cold ocean breezes that would otherwise reach the vineyards. Summers are warm, but rain is not unusual during harvests, making vintages vary extensively in quality. Graves is quite hilly, with many small, steep valleys cut out by the myriad small rivers and creeks. The soil in Graves is different than that found in most of the Bordeaux subregions. The steep vineyards have extremely gravelly soil, with large pebbles and stones overlaying a base of clay, sand, and some limestone. Important varieties include Merlot, Cabernet Sauvignon, Cabernet Franc, Sauvignon Blanc, and Sémillon.

The Libournais (Right Bank)

Some of the most prized Merlot-based wines are produced in the area around the town of Libourne on the right bank of the Dordogne River. Cabernet Sauvignon struggles in this region due to its continental climate and clay and limestone soil, ergo wines are primarily Merlot with a high percentage of Cabernet Franc.

One of the Libournais' most celebrated areas, Saint-Émilion borders the Dordogne River about eighty miles east of the town of Bordeaux. The village of Saint-Émilion has remarkably remained nearly unchanged since the Middle Ages. While the left bank (Medoc, Haut-Medoc, Graves) classification of 1855 has seen only one change in its entire history, the classification of the châteaux of Saint-Émilion is reviewed approximately once a decade. They were first classified in 1958 and placed in four categories: Saint-Émilion Premier Grand Cru Classé (A and B), Saint-Émilion Premier Cru Classé, and Saint-Émilion Grand Cru. However, there are only two appellations in the region: Saint-Émilion and Saint-Émilion Grand Cru. Although the classification is unrelated, it is still very important. The most famous of the premiers grands crus classé wines is Château Cheval Blanc.

Bordering Saint-Émilion to the west and the town of Libourne to the north is Pomerol. The wines of Pomerol are soft and velvety blends of Merlot and Cabernet Franc. The vineyards are planted in gravel with iron and clay. Its best producer, Château Pétrus, is consistently one of the most expensive wines in the world, although Pomerol has no classification system.

With a more continental climate than the majority of the Bordeaux subregions, the Libournais is warmer with less of a maritime influence. As with the rest of Bordeaux, the Libournais area is relatively flat, although some hills exist near Pomerol and Saint-Émilion. The clay and limestone soil here is ideal for Merlot, the blends of which are smooth and fruity, gaining incredible complexity with age. Although the region also produces Cabernet Sauvignon, it does poorly in this area. Cabernet Franc often supports the Merlot in the red blends.

RIGHT BANKS TO RELISH

Bordeaux and Bordeaux Supérieur: crisp, affordable dry white wines and high-value reds can be found carrying these appellation labels

Côtes-de-Bourg and Blaye: soft, fruity reds and basic whites from the Ugni Blanc grape; great values from underrated appellations

---

Burgundy

While Bordeaux is known for its history of commercial success, world-renowned châteaux, and bold, age-worthy wines, Burgundy (or Bourgogne in French) elicits a more emotional response from its admirers. Beyond their fabulously complex, delicious taste, there is a definite sensuality to Burgundian wines.

Apart from that, there are a few key differences between the regions. The first is ownership. While single families own most of the châteaux in Bordeaux, most Burgundian vineyards are divided among several owners. Due to inheritance laws implemented by Napoleon, small vineyards may have as many as a hundred owners. The result is an appellation system of such convoluted complexity that even learning how to read a Burgundian wine label can be quite a challenge. In addition, Burgundy produces less wine than Bordeaux, and the limited production means that acquiring specific bottles can be quite difficult. Although wines from Bordeaux are almost exclusively blends, wines from Burgundy are just the opposite. Burgundy red is always Pinot Noir; a white is always Chardonnay. Part of the reason Burgundy wines are so impressive is that they manage to coax subtle and complex flavors from a single grape.

A relatively small region in central eastern France, Burgundy has vineyards in the three *départements* of Yonne, Côte d'Or, and Saône et Loire, and it is divided into six appellations: Chablis, Côte Chalonnaise, Mâconnais, Beaujolais, Côte de Nuits, and Côte de Beaune, with the last two often grouped together as Côte d'Or.

Burgundy's climate is continental, entirely unmitigated by any bodies of water. Troubled by spring frost, summer hail, and fall rains, timing and weather are of the utmost importance in Burgundian viticulture.

Burgundy's chalky, mineral soil gives its wines intensely distinctive yet subtle flavors and aromas. Burgundy's Chardonnay is elegant, complex, and dry, with hints of nuts, butterscotch, flowers, fruit, minerals, and wet stone. Its Pinot Noir is medium-bodied and elegant, with aromas of earth and dark fruit flavors.

Chablis

Chablis is home to some of the driest and most elegant wines made from the Chardonnay grape. The region lies in the far north of Burgundy and is approximately forty miles closer to Champagne than it is to the rest of Burgundy. Although it is one of the classic regions of Burgundy, its growing conditions have more in common with Champagne than Burgundy. The cool weather presents challenges for growers, but excellent conditions produce a Chardonnay that is dry, crisp, and absolutely exhilarating.

Chablis's cold climate gives the grapes (and the resulting wines) searing levels of acidity. The northern European climate brings risk of frost and hail, and winters are usually quite cold. Spring is generally humid, and summer is hot and dry with an abundance of sunlight.

All seven of Chablis's grands crus lie on a single shelf of southwest-facing hillsides just north of the town of Chablis itself. The elevation of the vineyards is approximately five hundred feet, and one can see the picturesque town from the gently sloping hills of the grand cru vineyards. Most of Chablis's premiers crus, on the other hand, are on hillsides that slope southeast.

The soils of Chablis are composed of chalky clay with fossilized sea creatures. The combination of these Kimmeridgian and Portlandian soils, as they are called, and the cold, continental climate presents ideal conditions for the world's best Chardonnay wines. In fact, all Chablis AC wines are made from Chardonnay. There are forty premiers crus and seven grands crus in Chablis.

Traditionally, Chablis Chardonnay is unoaked, flinty, and steely with a greenish hue on the rim. It is more likely to find oak aging in wines of premier or grand cru status because their vineyards produce fruit that is ripe enough to stand up to the flavor of the wood, and they generally have more money to spend on expensive oak barriques. Aromas that whisper Chablis include hay, apples, minerals, and wet stone. Pinot Noir, Pinot Gris, and Sauvignon Blanc are grown to a lesser extent.

Côte de Nuits

The Cote d'Or, which means "golden slope," is a narrow strip of limestone soil divided into two sections: north of the city of Beaune is the Côte de Nuits, and the Côte de Beaune lies to the south. The Côte de Nuits is home to some of the world's most famous red wine producing vineyards and also produces a couple of great white wines as well. Of the twenty-three grand cru vineyards in Burgundy, twenty-two are in the Côte de Nuits. Simply put, the Côte de Nuits is the world's premier red wine district.

The Côte de Nuits is a contiguous area of vines that extends south from the city of Dijon to the northern edge of the Côte de Beaune. The climate here is mostly continental, with little influence from the Atlantic, meaning that winter is long and cold, spring is humid, and summer is hot with plenty of sun. The threat of hail is always present, and rain around the harvest can dilute the grapes and cause rot.

The Côte de Nuits is a small series of hillsides that runs along the famed RN 74 road at an elevation of 750 to 1,150 feet. The topsoil varies according to the altitude, although the base is limestone throughout. Nearly all the wine produced here is red, from Pinot Noir, which is known for its robust, silky, full flavors, although its Chardonnay is well known too.

CÔTE DE NUITS? CÔTE DE OUI!

Marsannay-la-Côte: most famous for its rosé wines, it has more recently been receiving acclaim for its reds

Fixin: robust, firm, and often tannic with good color; wines from this region, often excellent values, may also be labeled as Côte de Nuits-Villages

Gevrey-Chambertin: on the robust end of the Pinot Noir spectrum, but they have a silky elegance that those of Fixin typically lack

Morey-St-Denis: surprisingly not well known given the fact that it has four grands crus and part of a fifth, Bonnes Mares; the wines of Morey-St-Denis are feminine, rich, elegant, and complex

Le Musigny: comparable to the most famous of the vineyards in the Côte de Nuits, and its wines traditionally have a velvety, elegant texture

Flagey-Echezeaux: lighter and more delicate than their neighbors to the north

Grands Echezeaux: the best and most consistent vineyard site

Echezeaux: sometimes produces wines that are perhaps too light for their grand cru status

Vosne-Romanée: houses Burgundy's most famous vineyard, Romanée-Conti, which commands the highest price in Burgundy and is considered the best Pinot Noir in the world

Nuits-Saint-Georges: contains numerous premiers crus that produce delicious, full-bodied reds and several excellent whites

Côte de Beaune

The Côte de Beaune is a contiguous area of vines just south of the Côte de Nuits and extending further south, almost to the northern edge of the Côte Chalonnaise. Slightly more temperate and wetter than the Côte de Nuits, the Côte de Beaune faces less of a threat from hail. The biggest problems here are heavy rain and wet winds. The vines in the Côte de Beaune are planted on a series of east-facing hillsides at approximately one thousand feet. The slopes here are less steep than those in the Côte de Nuits and contain a flinty clay and calcareous topsoil that overlies a limestone subsoil with high iron content. The Chardonnay here is known for its rich, buttery, vanilla character, while the Pinot Noir is soft, delicate, fruit-driven, and generally a bit lighter in body than its cousin in the nearby Côte de Nuits.

The Côte de Beaune is really known for its complex, long-lived Chardonnay. Seven of the eight grand cru Chardonnay vineyards are found in the Côte de Beaune, and the rich white wines produced here are considered by many to be the best in the world.

CÔTE DE BEAUNE: A CLOSER LOOK

Aloxe-Corton: the best wines made within the commune are grand cru Chardonnay wines

Corton: the only red grand cru in the Côte de Beaune

Corton-Charlemagne and Charlemagne: the richest, most luxurious white Burgundies: both contain a rich, buttery, vanilla character

Savigny-les-Beaune: soft, fruity red wines

Pommard: quite well known and commercialized, and are often sold at higher prices

Volnay: specifically dedicated to reds, which are often characterized by floral, perfumed aromas.

St-Romain, Auxey-Duresses, and Monthelie: lighter-bodied whites and reds of a decent quality

Meursault: best known for its Chardonnay, characterized by its full body and flavors of hazelnuts and buttery spice

Le Montrachet: one of Burgundy's best grand cru vineyards, producing intense and luxurious nutty, creamy, toasty aromas

Côte Chalonnaise

About 220 miles southeast of Paris, between the Côte de Beaune to the north and Mâconnais to the south, Côte Chalonnaise enjoys a climate similar to that of the Côte d'Or, although a little dryer. Weather patterns spare the best slopes from frost and hail, and many of these provide ideal locations for viticulture. A region composed of small hills at elevations of one thousand feet, Côte Chalonnaise is rich in limestone. Because vines are generally grown on the best hillsides, the Côte Chalonnaise is a region of fairly sparse planting.

In comparison to the rest of Burgundy, the Côte Chalonnaise is easy to understand. Of its five wine appellations, two are purely white and three are red or white. Important varieties include Pinot Noir and Chardonnay. Chalonnaise wines are high in both quality and value, and although there are no grand crus here, there are quite a few premier crus. However, the term does not carry the same weight in the Côte Chalonnaise as it does in the Côte d'Or. Though high in quality, the wines rarely achieve the same kind of elegance and opulence as the Côte d'Or wines. Recently, however, the Côte Chalonnaise has built a reputation for quality wines, both red and white.

CÔTE CHALONNAISE: IN-DEPTH

Mercurey: best-known region in the Côte Chalonnaise, produces mainly medium-bodied, firm reds with earthy tannins and excellent color

Rully: excellent quality light, fruity red wines as well as rich, smooth whites

Bouzeron: only produces Aligote, which takes on a full fruity, spicy character similar in style to Pinot Gris

Givry: soft, medium-bodied Pinot Noirs

Montagny: Chardonnay similar in style to the wines of the Côte de Beaune

The Mâconnais

The Mâconnais produces large volumes of high-value Chardonnay. The majority of red wine that is produced there is made from Gamay, although it is rather unsuccessful in the limestone soil of the region. If you're scanning labels, a wine from Mâconnais is generally called "Mâcon." A Chardonnay from Mâconnais, for example, is called "Mâcon Blanc."

Mâconnais has a climate similar to the Côte Chalonnaise but experiences a more Mediterranean influence and is prone to the occasional storm. The north of Mâconnais is filled with the same rolling hills and gentle slopes as the Côte Chalonnaise. Farther from the Côte, however, you'll find steeper slopes and sharper hilltops as you approach Beaujolais to the south. The soil here consists of alluvium, clay, and sandy clay over a limestone base. Fresh and fruity with a crisp acidity, Mâcon Blancs are best enjoyed young.

Beaujolais

A huge, hilly region filled with sunshine at the southern end of Burgundy, Beaujolais produces the world's only classic Gamay wine. Even though Beaujolais produces fully half of Burgundy's wine, the distinct Gamay variety means Beaujolais should really be thought of as a region separate from the rest of Burgundy.

At the high end of the spectrum are the Beaujolais cru wines that earned Gamay's classic status. These are ten communes in the northeast of Beaujolais that have been given the distinction of being labeled by their commune name rather than as Beaujolais, or even the slightly better Beaujolais-Villages. At their best, these wines are fuller bodied with intense, ripe fruit flavor. The ten Beaujolais cru appellations are Brouilly, Chénas, Côte de Brouilly, Chiroubles, Fleurie, Juliénas, Morgon, Régnié, St.-Amour, and Moulin-á-Vent, the last of which is considered to be the best in the region.

Traditionally, Beaujolais is made using a vinification technique called carbonic maceration. The result is an extremely fresh and juicy style of wine. Although some wine is fermented in the traditional style, most Beaujolais undergoes at least a partial carbonic maceration.

Vines generally grow on sloping hills facing in any direction from 500 to 2,000 feet. The best vineyard sites in Beaujolais for the cultivation of Gamay are in the north, where there is a high level of granite in the soil. There are several levels of quality in Beaujolais ranging from the merely quaffable to the truly delicious and finely structured. To the south, the soil is rich in limestone. This presents a problem for the Gamay grape, and wines produced here lack the class of their northern cousins.

Loire Valley

The Loire Valley stretches across land dominated by the Loire River and produces a diverse range of wines. Dry whites dominate the eastern and western ends of the region, while a multitude of varieties appear in the center of the region.

The Loire is best known in the U.S. market for its white wines from Sancerre, Pouilly-Fumé, Vouvray, and Muscadet, but it also produces great reds, rosés, and sweet wines. Even though there are many styles of wine produced in the Loire, most of these wines have a distinct similarity in character. Today the Loire Valley is the only wine region in the world to specialize in Cabernet Franc, and it's the world's leading grower of Chenin Blanc.

The Loire is a sprawling wine region that extends hundreds of miles inland from the spot where the Loire River empties into the Atlantic. The topography is varied but remains low in altitude and includes valleys and gently sloping hills that protects vineyards from often chilling winds. In terms of terroir, the Loire divides into three subregions. Bordering the Atlantic coast is the mild and damp Pays Nantais, or Western Loire, an area that surrounds the city of Nantes. The area benefits from a maritime climate, although the winters can be harsh. The Middle Loire contains the regions of Anjou-Saumur and

Touraine, which have a more continental climate than the Western Loire, although rivers help to moderate the temperatures. Farther to the east are the Central Vineyards, which are cooler still.

The major grape variety in the Western Loire is the crisp Muscadet (also known as Melon de Bourgogne) that performs excellently when accompanied by Fruits de Mers or other seafood dishes. The principal white grape in the Middle Loire is Chenin Blanc, which is characterized by its full flavors and naturally high acidity. Chenin Blanc makes a range of wines: from dry to sweet and both still and sparkling. Although the Loire is best known for its white wines, the Middle Loire is also famous for its Cabernet Franc, which is made into dry red wines and rosés. The Central Vineyards to the east are home to the world-famous Sauvignon Blanc-producing regions of Sancerre and Pouilly-Fumé. This cool-climate region produces crisp wines with searing acidity that are occasionally mistaken for the wines of nearby Chablis.

Anjou-Saumur

It is in Saumur-Champigny that winemakers cultivate the Loire's best Cabernet Franc. The shale and gravel in the soil provide perfect conditions resulting in a very dry, full-bodied wine with a deep color, heavy tannins, and the ability to age well. Many believe this to be the Loire's finest red wine.

Anjou-Saumur lies just west of the Pays Nantais in central western France. Its vineyards lie mostly on the left (southern) bank of the Loire. The Atlantic influence is not quite so strong here as in the Pays Nantais to the west, but it still affects the area. The beneficial light rainfall and warm summers balance the unfortunate spring frost. Rolling hills hold back chilly winds from the west.

Anjou-Saumur is a large district with much soil variation throughout its vineyards. The soil in the Saumur-

Champigny is rich in gravel and shale, lending itself well to Cabernet Franc, while the chalkier soil around Saumur proper produces lighter wines, a haven for sparkling Chenin Blanc. Farther west, the soil is darker and either schist or clay, producing heavier wines and mostly non-sparkling Chenin Blanc.

Sparkling wines in Anjou-Saumur appropriate the Chenin Blanc's tartness, rendering it sweet and aromatic. To the west in Savennières, overripe Chenin Blanc produces succulent, long-lasting sweet wines, and to the east in Saumur-Champigny, grapes become full-bodied Cabernet Franc. In addition to Chenin Blanc and Cabernet Franc, the region is also known for its Gamay and Grolleau.

Central Vineyards

The name of this region is confusing at first because the Central Vineyards are not at all in the center of the Loire region. On the contrary, they mark its eastern edge. The Loire Valley, however, is a full six hundred miles long, and the Central Vineyards are far enough east to rest in the center of France.

This region is not as densely planted as the others in the Loire, and the vineyards are scattered widely across the countryside. Sauvignon Blanc is the area's variety of choice, and its striking aroma is arresting. A bit of Pinot Noir is grown, but the region is known for its Sauvignon Blanc, and its Pinot cannot compare to good Burgundy.

The Central Vineyards lie close to and southeast of Orléans in the center of France and mainly tend to follow the curve of the Loire River. The Central Vineyards are much farther from the Atlantic than the other regions in the Loire, and the climate is more continental as a result.

Vines are generally planted on hillsides in the river valley on sheltered, sunny slopes. The soil consists of a clay and limestone base, underlying gravel, and flinty pebbles. The chalkier regions produce lighter wines, while the regions rich in clay produce firmer, stronger Sauvignon. Sancerre and Pouilly are distinctive for their strong grassy aromas and sometimes a slight tang of cat urine—not a fault in this case.

Pays Nantais

The Nantais is synonymous for the dry, light-bodied white wine called Muscadet. The best Muscadet wines come from the Sévre-et-Maine district, an area that produces about 85 percent of all the Muscadet in the region. These wines are labeled as Muscadet de Sévre-et-Maine AC.

The generic Muscadet AC accounts for only 10 percent of production in the Nantais, even though it covers the entire area. Its wines are basic, dry, and light. Muscadet de Côteaux de la Loire AC lies on the Nantais' northern boundary along the coast and produces well-balanced wines of varying quality. Muscadet Côtes de Grandlieu AC, an appellation just to the west of Sévre-et-Maine, has offered wines with a nice fruity floral character since its establishment in 1994.

The Pays Nantais lies at the very western end of the Loire and stretches from the coast of the Atlantic inward. The close proximity of the Atlantic Ocean tempers the climate in Nantais.

The topsoil in the best vineyards in Nantais is light and stony, with sand and clay, while the subsoil is rich in minerals, schist, granite, and volcanic remnants. The Muscadet produced comes from a grape technically known as Melon de Bourgogne (melon of Burgundy), a crisp, fresh, and simple grape that pairs perfectly with the shellfish and seafood eaten in the region. The Muscadet in Sèvre-et-Maine in particular is less tart due to a higher clay content in the soil. Important wines of Pays Nantais include Muscadet and Folle Blanche.

Touraine

Touraine is a large region slightly east of the center of the Loire Valley. The vineyards fan out from Tours in a north-facing arc. Touraine is farther east than Anjou-Saumur and the Pays Nantais, with less of an Atlantic influence. Shielded from northerly winds by the Coteaux du Loir, the climate includes a warm summer and low rainfall in harvest season. The terrain in Touraine is rolling, as gentle slopes and idyllic hillsides stretch toward the horizon, with a flatter region around Tours itself. Vines are planted on the slopes between the low altitudes of 130 and 330 feet. Vouvray is known for the chalky tufa and limestone soil, ideal for tunneling and constructing cool underground wine cellars. In the more eastern Borgeuil and Chinon, the soil is sand and gravel. Wines from Borgeuil tend to be fuller, since that region has more clay in the soil, while wines from the more gravelly Chinon tend to be lighter. Important varieties include Chenin Blanc, Cabernet Franc, Sauvignon Blanc, and Grolleau.

The Northern Rhône

The Côtes du Rhône region as a whole is separated into three distinct quality levels: Côtes du Rhône, Côtes du Rhône-Villages, and Commune. Côtes du Rhône represents the most generic quality wine, though it can be a good value. Côtes du Rhône-Villages is much better as grape yields are required to be significantly lower. The Commune level is the best wine in the Rhône, and the labels will show the name of the particular region in which the wine was grown and produced. There is no system of rating wines, such as the grands crus or premiers crus in Bordeaux, but the system works well regardless since the top communes are quite well known.

The Northern Rhône is most famous for its deep colored Syrah blends, and it produces a few white and rosé wines as well. There are several important wine areas within the Northern Rhône appellation.

The Northern Rhone spans the distance from southern Burgundy to the Southern Rhône, following the Rhône River. The climate includes both Mediterranean influences and continental weather, giving the Northern Rhône hot summers and quite colder winters than its southern counterpart. Vineyards grow on steep sloping hills along the Rhône River on soil that is dry and light with granite, calcareous, and iron influences, the amount of which varies significantly by region. Important varieties of the area include deep, nearly black Syrah, the region's most famous export, and Viognier.

OTHER AREAS TO EXPLORE

Coronas: produces comparable Syrah to that of Hermitage but at a much lower price

Côtes-Rôtie: powerful reds, often Syrah blended with a small amount of Viognier

Crozes-Hermitage: red blends, peppery with lots of fruit

Hermitage: Northern Rhône's top red wines

St. Joseph: Syrah-based wines, best drunk young

Condrieu: incredibly fine, rare, and expensive white wines that do not age well

The Southern Rhône

In contrast to the tightly packed wine zone to the north, the southern Côte du Rhône's vineyards cover a broad circular expanse along the Durance River. Red wine dominates, with a few whites and rosés on the periphery. Grenache does particularly well on the warm hillside slopes. When comparing the Northern and Southern Rhône regions, the latter produces a remarkable 95 percent of the wine coming out of the Rhône region as a whole.

The Southern Rhone sprawls out across the lower part of the Rhône River and pushes south to the city of Avignon. The climate here has Mediterranean influences and continental weather, giving the Southern Rhône cooler summers and milder winters than its northern counterpart. Terrain is hilly, but slopes are less steep than in the north. Soil in the Southern Rhône is composed of stony topsoil interspersed with clay and limestone deposits, with areas of marl and pebbles. Important varieties of the region include Carignan, Cinsault, Grenache, Mouvedre, and Muscat, although the majority of wines are a blend of these.

REGIONS WITHIN THE SOUTHERN RHÔNE:

Chateauneuf-du-Pape: large volumes of wine at incredibly high standards, Chateuaneuf-du-Pape creates complex blends from Grenache, Syrah, and Mouvedre that age well

Coteaux de Tricastan: famous for its Syrah, Grenache, and Mouvedre blends as well as Gigondas; the red wines are a great pick for the price

Côtes du Lubéron: several red, white, and rosé blends; the rosés offer particularly pleasant, fruity flavors

Provence
Perhaps better known for its pleasant beaches and sunny weather, Provence is also home to some of France's top quality wines. Though nearly half of its grapes go toward the production of rosés, the most renowned of which are from the Bandol region, the reds of Provence offer deep flavors of spice and cassis that also typify the region. Within its borders Provence has several noteworthy appellations.

Much of Provence's modern wine history has been devoted to the production of rosés, but in recent years the region's red wines have taken a leading role. Located between the Languedoc region and the Italian border along the Mediterranean Sea, Provence boasts a climate that ranges from very hot summers and warm autumns to mild winters and springs. Rain is limited, and sunshine is abundant. Storms and cold winds originating over the Mediterranean do occasionally cause difficulties for wine-makers, but in general the region's climate is quite favorable for viticulture. Vines grow on dry hillsides and in more fertile valley floors. Soil here is diverse. Prevalent types are sand, sandstone, and granite, while some of the best locations have chalky outcrops of limestone. Top varieties of the region include Mouvedre, Cinsault, and Syrah.

EVEN MORE PLACES TO EXPLORE

Coteaux D'Aix-en-Provence: red blends dominated by Grenache, with Cinsault, Counoise, Mouvedre, and Syrah; excellent bottles can be found at both ends of the price spectrum

Côtes de Provence: known for rosés as well as high-end reds

Bandol: one of Provence's premier appellations most renowned for rosé wines

Bellet: offers the best whites in Provence

GERMANY

Key Taste

Riesling

Rieslings comprise some of the world's most elegant and aromatic white wines and have an extraordinary balance of sweetness and acidity with characteristic flavors of crisp apple (in the Mosel), apricot, peach and spice (in the Pfalz), lime, citrus, honey, flowers, spice, and marzipan characteristics.

Ask an average American what he or she thinks about German wine, and the odds are ten to one you will hear the words *sweet* and *white* in the answer. The sweetness myth is a common misconception with an easy explanation. During the 1960s and 1970s the majority of German wine that reached the United States was mediocre-quality, slightly sweet Liebfraumilch wine. The overabundance of Liebfraumilch led Americans to assume that all German wines were sweet; however, although Liebfraumilch is produced in Germany, no one in Germany drinks it. In fact, less than 1 percent of Germany's Liebfraumilch is consumed within German borders, and most of that is drunk by tourists.

Although Germany is certainly known for its dessert wines, the reality is that most German wines are dry or only slightly off dry, and generally of very high quality. Furthermore, the racy acidity of the Riesling grape makes low levels of residual sugar virtually undetectable on the palate.

The white wine myth is equally misguided, as almost a third of the grapes in Germany are red. Of those, a third are used to produce Germany's much-underrated Pinot Noir, called Spätburgunder. You don't hear about it very often, but a good Spätburgunder can rival the best French crus. And production is on the rise, with Spätburgunder gradually replacing some white varietals.

Germany's main variety, however, is and remains Riesling. Riesling accounts for 25 percent of German acres under vine, with an additional 20 percent occupied by Müller-Thurgau, an artificially created hardier cousin of Riesling. The best German Riesling pairs aromas of cream and peaches with a perfectly piercing acidity and can stand proudly alongside any white wine in the world.

Wine in the Land of Beer

The quality of German wine is unusually high for a counterintuitive reason: The Germans drink more beer than wine. Since beer is the drink of choice for everyday occasions, consumption of average-quality table wine is very low. In fact, the percentage of German grapes made into table wine hovers around 5 percent. This means the other 95 percent of German grapes are used in the production of high-quality wines. Compare this to France, where table wine represents the bulk of production.

Unlike France, Germany must contend with a thoroughly continental climate. With no nearby ocean to mitigate weather, the main wine regions in the southwest of the country must contend with widely varying temperatures from year to year. Not surprisingly, the vast majority of Germany's vines are planted along steep riverbanks. The river moderates climate where there is no ocean to do so; however, tending vines on the steep banks is incredibly labor intensive—another reason bulk wine is uncommon in Germany. Germany is unquestionably best known for its Riesling, which ranges from exceedingly dry to ambrosial dessert wine.

Rheingau

If Burgundy is the natural home of Pinot Noir, then the Rheingau is the abode of Riesling. Only here can Riesling achieve its full potential with lush, juicy, peach fruit flavors. This point is so well understood that many countries use the word *Johannisberg*, the village around which Riesling is grown in the Rheingau, to distinguish between true Riesling and lesser varieties. The impressive thing about Rheingau wines is that the honeyed character of the wine has nothing to do with noble rot or over-ripening; it simply comes from the terroir of the vineyards. With the natural taste of peach to recommend it, it should come as no surprise that the Rheingau is historically Germany's most successful wine region.

Although the temperatures in the Rheingau are relatively cool, vines are protected from the cold by the moderating influence of the Rhine and Main Rivers and by the

Taunus Mountains. Sunlight is plentiful, especially during the key months of May through October, and the south-facing slopes of vineyards here make the area marginally warmer than the Rheinhessen, which is further inland.

The vines grow entirely along the north slope of the Rhine and the Main Rivers. This south-facing slope runs for about thirty miles along the rivers and ranges from 330 to 985 feet in elevation.

Riesling loves slate, and the Rheingau delivers. Its best sites are located near the top of the slope and contain quartzite and weathered slate stone. Lower down, various soils of gravel, sand, clay, loam, and loess produce a less piercing but fuller style of wine. According to tradition, the blue phyllite-slate is thought to be ideal for Spätburgunder.

Wines from the Rheingau are said to be fuller and firmer than their cousins from Mosel. Some call the region's Riesling "muscular." Riesling accounts for nearly 80 percent of the wine produced in the Rheingau, and a mature Riesling from one of the high-ranking private estates here can call itself one of the best white wines in the world.

Mosel

The Mosel is Germany's westernmost wine region, following the Mosel River east from the French border. Mineral deposits along the 150-mile stretch of the Mosel give the wine here a distinct slate note called Schieferton. This minerality perfectly offsets the fresh fruit flavors in Mosel Rieslings.

Mosel can be divided into five regions: the Saar, Upper Mosel, the Ruwer, the Middle Mosel, and the Lower Mosel. In Saar, the village of Ockfen is known for the quality of its Rieslings and a soil so rich in slate that it forms a bluish dust on the fingers. In Upper Mosel, sparkling Sekt is what you'll want to try. Ruwer wines are riper and fruitier than the two just mentioned.

The Mosel River loops and wends its way toward France, almost never traveling in a straight line. The Riesling grape is often called "racy," referring to its high acidity. Mosel is cooler than the wine regions of the Rhine, producing fresh wines even in years so warm that the Rhine wines suffer. The region primarily produces Riesling and Müller-Thurgau.

Rheinhessen

In some respects, it is easy to generalize about Rheinhessen; in others, sheer variety makes it impossible. Rheinhessen is the most densely cultivated of Germany's wine regions, and it grows fully half the country's sweet Liebfraumilch. But beyond that, variety explodes. Riesling is the main grape here for quality wines, with hybrids like Müller-Thurgau or Schuerbe coming in next. Also, a full 8 percent of vines carry red grapes such as Spätburgunder or the widespread Portugieser. In addition, grapes here are increasingly being made into affordable sparkling Sekt.

The climate here is temperate, and the vineyards have several protections from the cold. The Taunus hills block winds from the north and the Odenwald forest blocks winds from the east. Vineyards sloping down to the river are protected from wind by the terrace itself.

The vineyards in the Rheinhessen occupy a large terrace southwest of a sharp bend in the Rhine. On the banks of the river, vines grow on east- and southeast-facing slopes. The elevation here ranges from about 300 to 600 feet. Farther from water the terrain is very different from Mosel or the Rheingau. The land here is flat, rolling, and endless, and vines lie on gentle slopes facing various directions. The soil here is incredibly varied but is mostly composed of loess left over from interglacial sandstorms. Other solids include limestone, marl, quartzite, silt, and clay. Reddish slate is widespread in the Rheinterrasse and gives the wine a distinct mineral edge.

Pfalz

The Pfalz is a region to watch in the next ten years. For decades, wine produced in the Pfalz was of mediocre quality, but recently the region has begun to demonstrate its potential for excellent wines.

Pfalz is run by small, independent farmers who produce a Riesling that is ripe, round, and high in alcohol. The Pfalz is sunny and dry, with shelter from the Haardt Mountains and the Donnersberg hills. The growing conditions here are considered so favorable that an incredible 93 percent of arable land in the region is devoted to vines.

Compared to the banks of the Mosel, the Pfalz is a tabletop plain. Vineyards here are situated either on flat land or on gently sloping hills. The altitude in the region ranges from 330 to 820 feet, though that change is more gradual than is characteristic of German wine regions. The soil is mainly loam, but loess, sand, sandstone, limestone, granite, and slate are also present. The Pfalz is known for its variety rather than any specialty, but it produces exceptionally good Riesling, Gewürztraminer, and Muskateller in addition to Müller-Thurgau.

Hessiche Bergstrasse

Hessiche Bergstrasse is a tiny wine region virtually unknown outside of Germany. Located just north of Baden, its terrain is very similar to those of the northern Baden region, and it shares northern Baden's preference for Riesling. The nearby Odenwald Mountains, however, offer such good protection that local vineyards are able to act as suntraps, making the average temperature the highest in Germany. Wines here are unusually dry for the country, with an excellent earthy acidity and a warm-weather peachiness that reveals the ripeness of the grapes at harvest.

Württernberg

Württernberg lies east of Baden on the sloping banks of the Neckar River. Like Mosel, the vineyards are very steep, but here most of them are terraced. The climate is continental, with spring and fall frosts posing the greatest threat to vines, but the growing season can also be very warm.

Württernberg has the distinction of being Germany's leading red wine producer, but its wine is mostly unknown. Light in body and in tannins, most of the wine produced is consumed in the area.

Baden

Although not as long as the Loire region in France, Baden is by far Germany's longest, extending from central southern Germany all the way south to the Swiss border. Baden was Germany's leading wine region throughout the nineteenth century but slowly declined into anonymity. Today Baden produces a few excellent estate wines that include some of Germany's very best reds, but these are mostly unknown outside the region. The bulk of production, however, is carried out by the Zentralkellerei Kaiserstuhler Winzergenossenchaften (ZBW), or Central Winery of Baden. The ZBW now accounts for 90 percent of the region's outputs and virtually all of its exports, but it is on the bland side and overshadows the excellent wines produced in Baden's best small vineyards.

Baden's climate is unusually sunny and warm for Germany due to the influence of the sheltering Black Forest and Odenwald Mountains. The land here is more level than in most German wine regions, and most vineyards are found on very slight slopes. Frost, however, can be a problem in low-lying areas, and some vines are planted high on hillsides to escape this threat.

Although Baden is more a collection of scattered vineyards than a unified region, there is a natural division into two parts. The section south of the town of Baden lies directly opposite the Alsace region just over the French border and shares Alsace's terrain. Müller-Thurau is the dominant grape here, but it is often blended with Silvaner and Riesling to make light wines for local consumption. As in much of Germany, however, Spätburgunder is on the rise. The warm temperatures here not only help Spätburgunder to ripen fully, they also lead to an unusually high alcohol content in Baden wine. Baden's northern region is cooler and rich in granite. Especially in the area around the old city of Heidelberg, the region produces some excellent Riesling with good acidity. The soil in the region is generally rich and fertile and includes gravel, limestone, clay, marl, loam, granite, and loess.

GERMAN GOODNESS

Mittelrhein: mainly producing Riesling, this underrated region is known for the high acidity of its wines, and it produces some excellent varietals

Ahr: Spätburgunder, or Pinot Noir, is the best-known variety here and covers nearly half the acreage, although Riesling is produced as well

Franken: Silvaner, usually used as a blending grape, is treated as a more noble varietal and makes its own distinctive wine with a dry earthy characteristic that, in the best wines, develops into smoky complexity

Nahe: grows mostly Müller-Thurgau, and it also produces some excellent, affordable Riesling

Saale-Unstrat and Sachsen: a wide variety of white varieties that are only going to get better

AUSTRIA

Key Tastes

Gewürztraminer, Grüner Veltliner, Pinot Gris,
Sauvignon Blanc, Chardonnay, Muscat-Ottonel

Austrian Gewürztraminer is a full-bodied and heavily scented wine, rich in alcohol. Grüner Veltliner is a white grape with great acidity, high sugar potential, and age-worthiness with peppery and spicy notes. Pinot Gris, a mutation of Pinot Noir, has the potential to be a super-rich, moderately aromatic white wine. Sauvignon Blanc from Austria has piercing aromas and crisp acidity. Muscat-Ottonel whites are lighter than those made from other Muscat grapes and often create a lovely dessert wine.

Although Austria has a history of red wine production, today it grows almost entirely white varieties. As a result of the cold climate, most of the grapes here are cold resistant and early ripening. Grüner Veltliner is the most widely known grape, with the hardy Swiss hybrid Müller-Thurgau coming in second. Riesling is grown only rarely, and red wines such as Spätburgunder, Portugieser, and Blaurer Zweigelt make up less than a tenth of production.

The antifreeze scandal of 1985, in which a few growers sweetened their dessert wines with a close chemical relative of automobile antifreeze, led to a complete overhaul of Austria's wine laws. Today they are modeled on the German system and are among the strictest in all of Europe. Each wine is classified by varietal, region of origin, and Prädikat, or sugar content. Like German wines, Austrian bottles are often referred to by their officially designated degree of sweetness—Spätlase is the driest quality wine and Trockenbeerenauslese is the sweetest.

History

Grapes in Austria have an ancient history. Celts planted vines as early as three thousand years ago, although it is not known whether they ever made wine. We do know, however, that viticulture grew under Roman occupation and flourished during the Middle Ages. Monasteries played a large role in winemaking, and monks themselves brought Pinot Noir and Riesling to Austria. Wine production reached its peak at the end of the Middle Ages, when Austrian vineyards covered an incredible ten times more land than they do today.

Austria was hit hard by phylloxera and a series of harsh winters at the end of the nineteenth century, but growers conducted continuous experiments aimed at producing hardier grapes. The main result was Grüner Veltliner, which represents the most important variety in Austria today. Although production had declined from its peak, the Austrian government passed a comprehensive new German-influenced wine law in 1972 and the industry was healthy moving into the 1980s.

Geography

Austrian vineyards are located entirely in the eastern half of the country, away from the Alps. The east is so far removed from the Atlantic, however, that the climate is continental with harsher and colder winters and hotter and dryer summers than in most of western Europe. More than half of Austria's wine comes from the large region of Niederösterreich, or lower Austria. The soil here is rich in shale, the Danube moderates temperature, and the Riesling is predictably excellent. More surprising are the 1,600 vineyards inside Vienna, Austria's capital. For historic reasons, Vienna is accorded status as its own wine region rather than as a part of Niederösterreich.

Although the winters can be harsh, the summers in Austria's wine region are generally warm, dry, and well suited to viticulture. In Burgenland, mists rising from the nearby Neusiedlersee create conditions ideal for noble rot.

Austria's wine territory is large and encompasses all forms of terrain. Vines are grown on steep riverbanks, on flat planes, on terraced valley walls, and on rolling hillsides. In the north the soil is mostly schist, limestone, and gravel. In the south there is more sand, with a high clay content in the volcanic region of Styria. Austria produces Grüner Veltliner, Müller-Thurgau, and smaller amounts of Chardonnay, Cabernet Sauvignon, and Merlot.

ITALY

Key Tastes

Nebbiolo, Barbera, Sangiovese, Malvasia Bianca, Gavi Gavi, Pinot Grigio, Dolcetto

Italian Nebbiolo bursts with earthy, complex flavors but can be so big and ferociously tannic that it requires years of bottle-aging before it's even approachable. Italian Barbera is highly acidic and often used in blends. Sangiovese is Italy's most planted variety and produces wines high in acid and tannin. Rich Dolcetto hails from northwestern Italy, where it is made into a dry, deep red wine with significant tannins, dark fruit, and pepper. In terms of whites, Italian Malvasia Bianca contains hints of honey and pear on the nose with a rich taste of fruit. Pinot Grigio, Italy's most iconic white grape, is often thought of as crisp and light but can be full and lush and extremely aromatic. Considered the best of Italy's white grapes, Gavi Gavi (also known as Cortese di Gavi) is crisp and boasts great minerality.

As essential as eating or sleeping, wine holds a special place in Italian culture. Its ubiquity alone proves its importance: Approximately one million producers grow nearly one thousand varieties of wine grapes. Over two million acres of vineyards spread across each region of the country, from the northern Alps to the southern island of Sicily. In addition, Italy possesses every possible microclimate desirable for the production of fine wine. From the cold, foggy mountains of Piedmont to the blazing heat of the south, Italy combines all the major wine-growing climates within a single country.

Italian Wine Today

Today Italian wine makes up about a quarter of the world's wine production. Year after year, Italy is France's closest rival as the largest producer and exporter of fine wines in the world, held back only by its confusing and loose system of appellations and quality control procedures.

East-Central Italy

The region of east-central Italy spans the distance from Molise in the south and almost to Piedmont in the north. East of the top of the Apennine Mountains, all of its subregions enjoy a pleasant Mediterranean climate, with fairly hot summers and cool winters. Most vineyards throughout east-central Italy grow on the many sloping hills, but viticulture has expanded on to the river valleys and plains in the more popular regions like Emilia-Romagna and the Abruzzi.

INCREDIBLE EAST-CENTRAL ITALY AT A GLANCE:

Emilia-Romagna: most popular varieties are Lambrusco, Trebbiano, and Albana, which produce very rustic whites, and the wines are exported worldwide

The Marches: well known for its dry Verdicchio white

The Abruzzi: Montepulciano d'Abruzzo, from Montepulciano and Sangiovese, stands out as a fabulous wine, but the remainder of the Abruzzi is fairly average

Molise: since there are no limiting factors in its climate, topography, or terroir, this coastal region ought to begin to live up to its potential

Northeast Italy

Bordered by Austria to the north and Slovenia to the east, this diverse section of Italy is home to the famous regions of Trentino-Alto Adige, the Veneto, and Friuli-Venezia Giulia. With the Alps in the north and the Adriatic Sea and the city of Venice in the south, topography, climate, and soil vary extensively throughout northeast Italy.

The Veneto

This region has become known as the Italian Bordeaux due to its excellent red blends. The Veneto, which produces the most wine in terms of volume in northeast Italy, is also, in good years, the number one producer in all of Italy. Though some of the Veneto's appellations have received criticism for their wine quality, most notably the areas of Soave and Valpolicella, new technology has lent some improvement. Visitors to the area are not limited to wine, nor is wine usually their focus—the picturesque city of Venice absorbs the majority of the region's tourism.

The Veneto's wines lined the walls of stores in the United States during the middle of the twentieth century. Imported mostly from Soave and Valpolicella, these inexpensive wines were mass-produced by large corporate bodies in Italy, making individual wines nearly indistinguishable.

As discussed in Chapter 4, Italy, like France, has a controlled appellation system with several levels of quality. Quality wines from defined regions are listed as Denominazione di Origine Controllata (DOC). A step above that is Denominazione di Origine Controllata e Garantita (DOCG), which follows stricter rules than DOC regions. There are now just over twenty DOCGs and the number is growing.

Small wineries lost their footholds as the traditional DOC boundaries of Soave and Valpolicella were exponentially expanded from the hills down into the flat alluvial plains. As a result of this expansion and overproduction, the Veneto's wines lost respect internationally and became known only for their mediocrity. Although there are many wineries producing great wines within Saove and Valpolicella, as well as other parts of the region, they remain overshadowed by the region's poor reputation.

Located north of Venice, the Veneto stretches around the land bordering parts of the Adriatic Sea. The Veneto is characterized by hot summers and cool winters, though tempered by its proximity to the Adriatic Sea. Most vineyards grow in the southern plains of the region, though many of the finest wines originate on surrounding hillsides. Silty, sandy soil prevails throughout the Veneto, with influences of clay and calcareous debris.

The region is known for its Soave, which is a light, simple white wine made from Garganega and Trebbiano. Although smooth and suave, it ought to be drunk within a few years of its vintage as it does not age well. Originally created in the hills covered with thick volcanic rock and soil, the area is now classified as Soave Classico DOC. The remaining area, which spreads into the plains below, is simply the Soave DOC. Soave Classico Superiore, an area with many good wineries that have made a real effort to save the overall region's name, was recently honored by receiving the DOCG title.

Bardolino is another light wine made from Corvina, Molinara, and Rondinella, with Corvina composing the majority of the blend. While the Bardolino Classico DOC is better than simple Bardolino, the best wine is made in the Bardolino Superiore DOCG.

Valpolicella is a blend of at least 70 percent Corvina with added amounts of Molinara and Rondinella. This wine tends to be smoky with strong cherry flavors. As with the above regions, Valpolicella Classico DOC and

Valpolicella Classico Superiore improve upon the wine from the basic classification.

Other regional wines include Amarone and Prosecco. An intensely aromatic wine, Amarone possesses a very full body. The wine is made from partially dried grapes, and the long fermentation process creates a high alcohol content within this wine. Prosecco is a Frizzante produced just outside of Venice, extremely popular in the Veneto region.

Trentino-Alto Adige

Almost completely covered by mountains, Trentino-Alto Adige combines Italian and German traditions. German is spoken in the north of the region, in Bolzano, and wines are named in both Italian and German. Vineyards are generally at high elevations and bear the influences of a cool climate and gritty, stony soil. Chardonnay, imported from France hundreds of years ago, is the most important variety here and is used to produce the sparkling Spumante. There are twelve DOC subregions within Trentino-Alto Adige, the most important being Alto Adige DOC, Santa Maddalena, Trentino, and Teroldego Rotaliano. Teroldego produces the region's best red wine, which is full-bodied and ages well, while Alto Adige makes excellent Schiava.

Following World War II, both rapid industrialization and the development of tourist routes in the region spurred Trentino-Alto Adige's wine economy, and it continues to grow slowly. Though the region only produces a tiny percentage of Italy's total amount of wine, the quality remains quite high.

The northernmost wine region in all of Italy, Trentino-Alto Adige pushes up against Austria in the north. Summers are fairly warm, but winters are very cold. The climate varies extensively from year to year, making vintage selection important. Vineyards grow on steep slopes in the mountainous landscape of the region where wine is produced at altitudes of over 3,000 feet. Soil is generally rocky with influences of clay, sand, and sometimes calcium. The light earth of northern Trentino-Alto Adige suffers from leaching, making fertilization a necessity.

The region produces Chardonnay, which is frequently mixed with Pinot Bianco to produce very good Spumante; a Pinot Grigio full of flavors of melon, quite round, and smooth; Müller-Thurgau; and a medium- to full-bodied Schiava with flavors of black fruits and licorice.

Friuli-Venezia Giulia

Situated in the mountainous northeast corner of Italy, Friuli-Venezia Giulia produces some of Italy's finest whites. Bordering Slovenia in the east, this region has some Slavic influences within its wine culture. For example, Tocai Friulano, the region's most popular variety, may have originated in eastern Europe and bears a Slavic name (Tocai). Other good white varieties are Sauvignon Blanc, Pinot Grigio, and Pinot Bianco, and popular reds include Schioppettino, Refosco, Merlot, Cabernet Sauvignon, and Cabernet Franc. Friuli-Venezia Giulia has a reputation for putting quality ahead of quantity and has earned its place as one of the top regions in Italy.

The climate here consists of warm days, cool nights, strong maritime breezes, and humidity, which is tempered by cool air off the mountains to the north. There is an average amount of rain. Vineyards are grown on the plains extending from the foothills to the Adriatic Sea. Soil is rocky and calcium-rich in the foothills and alluvial and sandy on the lower plains.

The region produces a variety of wines, both red and white, and dessert wines. The Pinot Grigio contains hints of almonds, peaches, and pears on the nose, with a fruity flavor and strong acidity. The aromatic Sauvignon Blanc has hints of herbs and is fairly acidic, while the Tocai varies between lush and spicy depending upon the producer. Pinot Bianco is also produced. For the reds, both the Merlot and Cabernet Sauvignon are light and fruity, while the Schioppettino is strong and spicy with intense cherry flavors. The Ramandola is a sweet and golden dessert wine with aromas and tastes of honey and dried fruit.

Piedmont

Piedmont, or *Piemonte* in Italian, means "the foot of the mountains." An apt name given its location at the base of the Alps, Piedmont enjoys a cool continental climate with a hot growing season and quite foggy conditions. The great Nebbiolo wines of Piedmont are named for this fog, or *nebbia*. The cuisine of the region is often rich and creamy with lots of meat, risotto, and the famous white truffles (tartuffi bianchi).

Piedmont produces more wine than any other Italian region and makes the highest percentage of quality wines in Italy. Piedmont is home to some of the most robust, long-lived wines in the world, many of which are indigenous to Piedmont and rarely excel anywhere else in the world. In particular, the wines of Barolo and Barbaresco are two of Italy's best. Like fine Bordeaux, these Nebbiolo wines take years of aging before they can be drunk. When they are young, they are viciously tannic, but with proper cellaring they have the potential to become extraordinary.

Pressing up against France and Switzerland, Piedmont is located in the northwestern corner of Italy. Severe winters and warm summers characterize the region, and frequent mountain fogs add an additional dimension of complexity. Hail is not unusual and can damage harvests during the long ripening period of many of Piedmont's grapes. Vineyards grow predominantly along moderately steep hillsides, though some have spread into the river valleys below. Soil is composed largely of calcium-rich marl, sand, and clay, but the actual composition varies extensively.

One important variety is the rich and flavorful Barbera, which requires less aging than Nebbiolo. Moscato is used mostly to make Spumante or Frizzante, which can be luscious and sweet or dry. The best of Piedmont's white wines are made from Muscat Blanc à Petits Grains, the highest-quality grape in the Muscat family. One of the most important of these wines is the sparkling Asti DOCG, which is naturally sparkling and slightly sweet with a low level of alcohol. Another similar wine is the delicious, slightly sparkling Moscato d'Asti DOCG. Moscato d'Asti averages about 5 percent alcohol and usually has a distinct grapelike aroma in its youth.

Rich and smoky in Barolo, elegant and feminine in Barbaresco, Nebbiolo—however it is expressed—is an important grape in Piedmont. Aging is required for the traditionally made Nebbiolos. Barolo producers are divided into two camps: those who vinify in the traditional manner and those who use modern techniques.

Traditionally the wine is left in contact with the skins for long periods of time during fermentation and aged in large oak or chestnut casks for years. These traditional-style Barolos are complex and earthy with flavors of tar, truffle, violets, tobacco, prunes, and smoke. In the modern style, winemakers focus their efforts on softening the Nebbiolo grape's harsh tannins and on extracting the maximum color.

The main difference is that in the modern style, wines are aged in small, new oak barriques for little longer than the required two years. In this style, the wines tend to be softer with a vanilla character and are generally ready to drink years earlier than the wines made in the traditional style.

Wines made from the Dolcetto grape are smooth and quaffable but should generally be consumed when young.

Northwest Italy

Encompassing an incredibly diverse geographical area, the northwest section of Italy covers the distance from France in the west to Veneto and Trentino-Alto Adige in the east. Within this northwest corner lie some of Italy's top wine regions, which produce such wines as rich Piedmont Nebbiolos and delicious sparkling Spumantes.

INCREDIBLE ITALY: TAKE TWO

Valle d'Aosta: Italy's smallest region, which often labels its wines in French

Liguria: mainly consumed by locals due to its tiny production

Lombardy: most densely populated region in Italy, home to Valtellina (most northern producer of Nebbiolo), Franciacorta (try their sparkling wines!), and Otrepo Pavese (largest production, has every type of wine imaginable!)

Southern Italy

It seems that vineyards have always been a part of southern Italy's scenic landscape. Its hot, dry climate make southern Italy well suited for dark, alcoholic wines of which it produces a seemingly limitless amount. Indeed, for much of modern history the region was known only for its bulk production booze. But to write off southern Italy so quickly would be a mistake, since outside the vast industrial producers many smaller wineries make some extremely good and very expressive wines.

INCREDIBLE ITALY: TAKE THREE

Campania: has produced great wines like Taurasi, a red made from Aglianico grapes, and some fine white wines—Greco di Tufo and Fiano di Avellino—but also tends to overproduce without thought to quality

Apulia (Puglia): the heel of the Italian "boot" on a map; the region is gaining great recognition for the ancient Aglianico, the Zinfandel-like grape indigenous to the region, as well as Primitivo

Basilicata: as is the case from Puglia, the best wines from the region are those made from both Aglianico and Primitivo; delicious cheeses (like ricotta) are also Basilicata's claim to fame

Sardinia: the region's famous wines, Cannonau di Sardegna DOC and Vermentino di Gallura, use varieties from Spain; these include the Cannonau grape (the equivalent of Spain's Garnacha) and the white Vermentino grape

Sicily: Sicily's claim to fame is its fortified Marsala wine (look for Vergine, the name given to the finest Marsala)

West-Central Italy

Lying between the Apennine Mountains and the Mediterranean Sea, west-central Italy is a crucial region for Italian wine. Most famous for the wine region of Tuscany (and the Chianti wines from within Tuscany), west-central Italy also encompasses the wine regions of Latium and Umbria as well as the Italian capital city of Rome.

Tuscany

One of Italy's top wine producers, the region of Tuscany is rivaled in prestige only by Piedmont. Tuscany contains a number of very fine DOC and DOCG appellations within its geographical borders and is the home to some very good Super Tuscan wines. For more on Super Tuscans, see Chapter 4.

Chianti is by far the most important Tuscan appellation. Chianti is in the heart of Tuscany, centrally located within the region. Of Tuscany's 157,000 acres of vineyards and 57 million gallons of wine, almost half of it is from Chianti. Much is exported to the United States, the majority of which is pleasant wine meant for immediate drinking. However, Chianti Classico and Chianti Classico Superiore DOCGs can produce some incredible wines that compete at the highest level. Chianti Riservas are particularly fine, coming from warm, dry vintages. These conditions transform the wine, giving it layers of ripe plums and cherries, earth, truffles, and other complexities. Many of these top Chiantis will age for over twenty years.

Chianti shares Tuscany with Brunello di Montalcino DOCG and Vino Nobile di Montepulciano DOCG, both of which produce wines of great quality. Brunello is a local variety of the Sangiovese grape, which makes wines so thick and harsh that they should age at least ten to twenty years before opening.

Located just north of Rome, Tuscany expands north along the Apennine Mountains. The climate of Tuscany is warm and fairly dry with mild winters and hot, dry summers. Vineyards grow on sloping hillsides to provide good sun exposure and drainage. Due to the hot summers, winemakers plant heat-sensitive grapes at higher altitudes with cooler air and breezes. Soils are complex, with the best containing a unique rocky blend called galestro. Important varieties are Sangiovese (also known as Brunello), Morellino, Prugnolo, Sangioveto, Tignolo, and Uva Canina. Other varieties grown are Malvasia and Trebbiano, which is also known as Procanico.

Umbria

Located east of Tuscany and north of Latium, Umbria produces the well-known but mediocre Orvieto wine but also makes an excellent wine in the Torgiano DOC appellation and the Torgiano Riserva DOCG. The latter wine is made with many different grapes, both from France and from Italy.

Latium

Latium, also known as Lazio, makes only a few fine wines (Boncompagni Ludovisi's Fiorano Rosso and Cantina Colacicchi's Torre Ercolana—Cabernet Sauvignon-Merlot blends). The region's main focus is in the production of the hugely popular though mediocre Frascati, Latin Liebfraumilch, and Est! Est!! Est!!! wines. This region is located south of Tuscany and Umbria with Rome at its center.

SOUTH AFRICA

Key Tastes

Chenin Blanc, Pinotage, Bordeaux blends, Shiraz, Chardonnay, Sauvignon Blanc

Most consumers have a love-hate relationship with South Africa's indigenous Pinotage. Pinotage is a grape created from the cross of Pinot Noir and Cinsault. Created in South Africa in the 1920s, Pinotage is often characterized by a smoky character and occasionally by a bitter taste.

The story of winemaking in South Africa paints a broader picture of the country's history. Wine production, like the modern state, began with Dutch colonization, grew throughout British rule, faltered in a twentieth century of apartheid and isolation, and enjoyed a renaissance with the defeat of the entrenched National Party in the election of 1994.

History

Winemaking in South Africa begins with Simon van der Stel, commander of the Dutch colony at the Cape of Good Hope. In 1685 van der Stel planted his first vines, naming the site after his benefactor's daughter. With its fertile soil, sloping hills, and ocean breezes, Constantia's growing conditions were near perfect. For the next two hundred years, this would be South Africa's grand cru. Despite its limited circulation, the sweet, red dessert wine, simply titled "Constantia," was well known in high society across Europe. Napoleon himself specifically requested Constantia during his exile at St. Helena, and British writers such as Dickens and Austen sang its praise.

Outside of Constantia, however, South Africa's wine industry struggled. Early efforts in the nearby Stellenbosch and Paarl faced heavy government regulation and a variety of difficulties. By 1812, the Cape's wine industry had entered its heyday as British import duties favored African wines over those of the French due to the Napoleonic wars. But bad weather and a ruined crop in 1825 marked the beginning of a steady slide, and Britain gradually began to raise tariffs on wine from the Cape. In 1859, mildew devastated the vines, and in 1886, phylloxera aphids took a heavy toll. Although Cape winemakers followed the example of their European counterparts, planting new vines grafted onto resistant American rootstock, the industry was decimated by the effects of the Boer War (1899–1902).

South African winemaking in most of the twentieth century was synonymous with the Co-operative Winegrowers Association of South Africa, or KWV. Founded in 1918, the KWV aimed to defend farmers through collective bargaining. Within years, it had imposed a minimum price on wine and guaranteed farmers that it would buy up excess wine. Unfortunately, the KWV's policies valued quantity over quality, and South African wine, already disadvantaged by international antiapartheid trade sanctions, suffered as a result.

Due to the effects of the election of 1994, namely the end of apartheid and the victories of Nelson Mandela and the African National Congress, the trajectories of the country and the wine industry dramatically improved. In a few short years, the KWV was stripped of the bulk of its regulatory power and Cape wine farmers were thrust into a free market. Exports shot up, négociants sprang up overnight, and many of South Africa's wine cooperatives soon became proprietary companies with shareholders.

The real success stories of the new system have been small boutique wineries. Now spread across the Cape, clustering in the booming Stellenbosch district, the wineries have greatly improved the quality and reputation of South African wines. Today South Africa is a land of excitement and experimentation as growers plant a variety of grapes to determine the best pairings between variety and terroir. Although the multifaceted country has yet to produce a distinctive specialty, it has built a reputation for its Pinotage, Cabernet Franc, Cabernet Sauvignon, Chardonnay, and Chenin Blanc.

Constantia

Home to the first vineyard at the Cape, Constantia occupies a special place in the lore of South African winemaking. Although it has never produced more than 3 or 4 percent of South Africa's wines, Constantia has historically been responsible for the country's best-regarded bottles.

Constantia enjoys a mild Mediterranean climate with generous winter rainfall. Ocean air off the nearby False Bay helps keep temperatures mild, and occasional rain and Atlantic breezes moderate warm summers. A suburb of Cape Town, Constantia is a ward inside the Coastal Region of South Africa. Its vineyards lie on the gentle slopes at the foot of Constantia Mountain, and its south-facing hillsides offer spectacular views of the nearby False Bay. Stellenbosch, Paarl, and Durbanville all lie nearby to the northeast. Vineyards in the area adorn the mountain foothills, running parallel with the beaches of the popular False Bay, and must now compete for space with housing developments in Cape Town's affluent residential suburbs.

The soil varies with elevation as you climb the mountain slopes, but it is mostly granite-based and contains large amounts of clay. Constantia is particularly known for its Sémillon, Muscat, Sauvignon Blanc, Chardonnay, Cabernet Sauvignon, Shiraz, and Pinot Noir.

Paarl

The district of Paarl is named after a large dome-shaped rock formation within its borders. The granite rocks on this peak shine and sparkle in the sunlight, leading the first Dutch explorers in the region to name the mountain "den Diamant ende Peerlbergh," the Diamond and Pearl Mountain.

Paarl lies in the Berg River Valley, bordered by the Paarl Mountains and the Drakenstein Range. It lies to the north of the famous Stellenbosch district and about forty miles northeast of Cape Town. Similar to the Rhône Valley in southern France, the warm summers and wet winters in Paarl make it well suited to the production of fine wines. Summer runs from October through March, with warm weather tempered by cool Atlantic breezes prevailing during the harvest season. Winter is colder but moderated by the relative proximity to the ocean. The high mountains surrounding the district trap the winter clouds, dropping enough rain to maintain the vineyards with a minimum of irrigation.

The vineyards grow on the flat valley floor and have expanded extensively into the surrounding hillsides. There are three distinct soil types in the Paarl district. The mountain slopes are composed of granite-based soil and as such have very good drainage. The fertile Berg River Valley contains a soil blend of primarily Table Mountain sandstone. Shale is interspersed throughout the northeastern corner of the district. The district produces Shiraz, Viognier, Mourvèdre, Cabernet Sauvignon, Sémillon, and Chardonnay.

Stellenbosch

Today accepted as South Africa's greatest wine district, Stellenbosch has become world famous for its high-quality estates. Stellenbosch lies in a river valley between high mountains. The soil is made of granite along the mountain slopes, as well as sandstone and shale with good water retention. The river valley soil is extremely fertile and contains pockets of the Hutton soil, which the winegrowers love. The particularly granite-rich regions provide ideal growing conditions for red wines, while the areas with a higher concentration of sandstone-based soil produce excellent whites.

Nestled between coastal mountain ridges, Stellenbosch enjoys a pleasant Mediterranean climate ideal for growing high-quality grapes. Summer runs from October through March, with warm weather tempered by cool Atlantic breezes prevailing through the harvest season. Winter is cool and rainy but moderated by the proximity to the ocean. The vineyards grow on the flat valley floor and have expanded extensively into the surrounding hillsides. The valley's altitude is about 300 feet.

The region's best-known wines come from distinct appellations. Jonkershoek Valley, located east of Stellenbosch town, is famous for its Cabernet Sauvignon and Cabernet blends. Simonsberg-Stellenbosch, in the southwestern foothills of Simonsberg Mountain, produces high-quality Cabernet Sauvignon, Cabernet blends, Pinotage, and other reds. To the northwest of Stellenbosch town, Bottelary is well regarded for its Pinotage, Shiraz, and other warm-blooded blends. Devon Valley, northwest of Stellenbosch town, primarily makes red blends. Papegaaiberg, to the west of Stellenbosch town, contributes Chardonnay, Chenin, Merlot, and Cabernet Sauvignon.

The rest of the Stellenbosch region, which remains unappellated, is well known for red blends, Chenin, and Sauvignon Blanc. Throughout Stellenbosch, one can find Merlot and Chardonnay vines as well.

Franschhoek

Known as the Wine and Food Capital of the Cape, Franschhoek is a small but important wine region of South Africa. Located just east of Stellenbosch, Franschhoek enjoys a warm climate tempered by relative proximity to the ocean; however, the coastal mountains provide a sheltering influence, making Franschhoek slightly warmer than its neighbor. The most popular varieties produced here are Sauvignon Blanc, Chardonnay, Sémillon, Chenin Blanc, Cabernet Sauvignon, Shiraz, Pinot Noir, and Merlot.

SUPERB SOUTH AFRICA

Robertson: the "valley of wine and roses," with famous Riesling, Cabernet Sauvignon, Sauvignon Blanc, and Chardonnay

Swartland: bold, powerful reds and lush white wines compose the majority of styles produced

Walker Bay: areas within Walker Bay include Elgin and Hemel-en-Aarde, which arguably produce the best Pinot Noir in South Africa

ISRAEL

Key Tastes

Muscat, Riesling, Sauvignon Blanc, Cabernet Sauvignon, and Merlot

Wines made from Muscat are quite sweet and distinctive. Honeylike, the grape is also purchased as grapes or raisins for eating. Riesling makes some of the world's most elegant and aromatic white wines with an extraordinary balance of sweetness and acidity plus citrus, honey, flowers, spice, and marzipan. Sauvignon Blanc has piercing aromas and crisp acidity.

Though a recent and still quite small player in the international wine market, Israel has proven itself worthy of comparison with any New World country. Once known only for its sweet religious wines, the country now boasts a wide variety of award-winning table wines as well. Israel's viticulture is divided into five separate geographical regions: Galilee, the Judean Hills, Samson, Negev, and Shomron.

History

Israel's history with wine is long and involved. Legend holds that when Moses and the Israelites arrived at Palestine, two spies returned from what is now Israel carrying a cluster of grapes. According to biblical history, the wine from these grapes lasted for forty years as Moses and his followers wandered the deserts of the Sinai Peninsula.

We do know that Israel exported wine to the Egyptians and later to the Roman Empire. Not known for their quality, these Israeli wines were incredibly sweet, unsophisticated, and strong. With the waning of the Byzantine Empire, Israel was conquered by the Islamic Empire in A.D. 636 and winemaking effectively stopped for over a thousand years.

Although Baron Edmond de Rothschild, prominent in France's wine industry, reintroduced viticulture to the region in 1870 by providing financial support and sending winemaking consultants, the wine retained its sickly rich and medicinal taste. Israeli independence in 1948 did little to change the country's wine, which was still used mostly for religious ceremonies.

In the 1980s Israel's winemaking culture took a dramatic leap forward with the production of fine table wines for daily consumption. Thanks to influences from France and California, several wineries began to win notable international awards. The trend of rapid improvement has continued to this day, and Israel's several climate zones have contributed to making Israeli wines as diverse as they are good.

INTRIGUING ISRAEL

Galilee: arguably the finest wine region in Israel with its high altitude, cool sea breezes, and well-draining soil, Cabernet Sauvignon, Chardonnay, Merlot, and Sauvignon Blanc are produced

Judean Hills: this area's high climate and cool temperatures make it well suited to varietals like Chardonnay, though it also produces much of Israel's sweet wine for religious ceremonies

Samson: lies between the coastal plain of central Israel and the Judean Hills to the east

Negev: a recent addition to Israel's wine map, the Negev region lies in the hot, dry desert to the south and requires extensive irrigation to produce Cabernet Sauvignon and Merlot

Shomron: located in northwestern Israel around the city of Haifa, it benefits from a distinctly Mediterranean climate

LEBANON

Key Tastes

Obaideh, Merwah, Cabernet Sauvignon, Cinsault, Carignan

Indigenous to Lebanon, Obaideh has been linked to Chardonnay. Merwah, also indigenous to Lebanon, is very much like Sémillon. Cabernet Sauvignon often has high levels of phenolic compounds, leading to good tannin and structure. Cinsault, with its subtle blue fruit, spice, and nuts, is particularly popular in the creation of rosé. Carignan is a harsher, full-bodied red grape that is used to support the structure and density of blends.

Although considered among the New World producers, Lebanon was producing wine even before the ancient Greeks. In fact, the Bible mentions Lebanese viticulture and records Lebanon as the place where Jesus turned water into wine. Lebanon's recent past has been infinitely more troubled, but winemakers succeed in producing award-winning products. Wine production exists throughout the country, particularly in the eastern Bekaa Valley, where the vines bask in three hundred days of sunshine per year.

History

The ancient Phoenicians began to make wine in Lebanon as early as 3000 B.C. Great travelers and explorers, they proceeded to spread viticulture around the entire known world: from Greece to Spain to Northern Africa. However, their weak military abilities led to their domination by other empires, including the Egyptians, the Assyrians, the Babylonians, the Greeks, the Romans, the Arabs, the French, and the Ottomans. In point of fact, the region has only sporadically been independent since the beginning of Lebanon's recorded history. Despite its most recent independence in 1943, Lebanon underwent a brutal civil war from 1975–1990.

Today not only must Lebanese wineries worry about traditional issues like drought, frosts, and disease, but they also have to cope with Syrian tanks, local rebels, and the occasional Israeli jet. Remarkably, a few winemakers have managed to persevere, and Lebanon has gained a hard-earned reputation for producing a few extremely fine wines, particularly those of Château Musar.

Geography

Lebanon is located along the eastern coast of the Mediterranean Sea, with Israel to the south and Turkey to the north. The climate is warm, though the nearby Mediterranean and the inland mountains both have cooling effects.

Lebanon's vineyards are best known for their remarkably sunny climate, with over three hundred days of sunshine per year; however, the high altitude of the valley significantly lowers temperatures at night. Vineyards grow mostly on the slopes and flat lands in the Bekaa Valley at elevations of up to 3,200 feet, on soils that are predominantly gravel-based, and are underlaid by a thick layer of limestone.

The important varietals in Lebanon include Cabernet Sauvignon, Carignan, Chardonnay, Chasselas, Cinsault, Clairette, Gamay, Grenache, Muscat, Obaideh, Pinot Noir, Riesling, Sémillon, Syrah, and Ugni Blanc. Many of Lebanon's best wines are red blends with an emphasis on Cabernet Sauvignon. Lebanon's indigenous grape varieties are Obaideh, which has been linked to Chardonnay; and Merwah, akin to Sémillon.

INDIA AND CHINA

Key Tastes in India

Shiraz, Chenin Blanc

Shiraz, also known as Syrah, creates bold, peppery wines. Chenin Blanc can produce a variety of wines—the best have lots of sugar and acidity.

Indian wine is enjoying a rise in popularity. Globalization has led to increased demand for wine, while the government has recently tangled with the World Trade Organization over the taxes on imports. The answer? India's burgeoning wine industry, which currently creates 1.3 million cases of wine a year.

Although wine has not existed in India quite as long as China, it does date to the sixteenth century, a pedigree far longer than any of the New World wines. Under the British Empire, however, whiskey took the place of wine and has remained the alcohol of choice. Today, though, the image of wine as cosmopolitan, classy, and healthy has led to its increased popularity, and its inclusion in certain Bollywood films imply that wine in India is here to stay.

Wineries to Watch

* Sula-Rajeev Samant, CEO of Sula Vineyards, is a graduate of Stanford University and has been called the Jess Jackson (of Kendall Jackson) of India.

Key Tastes in China

Chardonnay, Cabernet Sauvignon

As is the case with many products, luxury brands of wine, particularly American and French, have been imported into China for decades. The challenge with these luxury brands in China becomes authenticity. Rumor has it that faux bottles of great French and American wines have been saved and far lower-quality wines have been poured into them, akin to knockoff Louis Vuitton purses.

Although wine has been produced in China for the past thousand years, it has only recently exploded onto the world market—and even its own culture! Although still not a part of the daily life of the average Chinese citizen, Chinese who have been educated in the West have begun to consider understanding wine a symbol of status.

China is best known for producing Chardonnay. Hua-dong, one of the older wineries in China, was started by Michael Parry in the mid-1980s and was the first to produce noble grapes. Three-quarters of its production are consumed within China. It is held back by the lack of availability of grapes as only 160,000 acres of vines are available in the country and they are difficult to access.

First mentioned in 138 B.C., wine has recently spread across the country in part due to a decision by the Communist Party in 1987 to switch from grain liquor to fruit liquor. Between 1996 and 2002, over one hundred domestic wineries opened, many producing Chardonnay and Cabernet Sauvignon. Producing 300,000 tons of wine per year, the consumption is higher than the creation, leading to a significant amount of imported wine, mainly from France, Italy, and Spain, and some from the Napa Valley.

Distribution Channel to Watch for Chinese Wine

* *Chinese restaurants in the United States.* When they start importing Chinese wines, watch out, Tsingtao beer.

AUSTRALIA

Key Tastes

Sauvignon Blanc, Chardonnay, Shiraz, Cabernet Sauvignon, Cab-Shiraz blends

Syrah creates peppery wines in general; in Australia, Barossa Valley Shiraz are iconically bigger, bolder, riper, more syrupy, more chocolaty, and sometimes more tobacco-y in flavor than their French counterparts. Sauvignon Blanc from Australia often has bright acidity and delightful aromas.

Australia's wine production has skyrocketed in the last twenty years, and vineyards now grow in every location where the climate allows viticulture. From the baking heat of the Swan District in the west to the cool, rainy island of Tasmania, Australia's wines span the broadest spectrum.

Australia's fame has deservedly risen from its big, bold reds produced mainly from Shiraz and Cabernet Sauvignon. Enjoying warm weather and ideal soil conditions, these wines, particularly from Coonawarra, Barossa Valley, and McLaren Vale, achieve incredible flavors and intensity. However, Australia does much more than just produce these powerful wines. Yarra Valley in Victoria, for example, is home to some of Australia's finest Pinot Noir, which rivals that of Burgundy itself. The Hunter region in New South Wales is famous for its unique, crisp Sémillon. To sum up the country in a single phrase, Australia offers a multitude of fine wines whose relatively low price will force competing countries to shape up or get out.

History

Wine production in Australia began in 1788 at the settlement of Farm Cove in New South Wales. The first governor of the then British colony, Captain Arthur Phillip, planted vines of Brazilian origin in the fertile soil on his way to Sydney. Later, realizing the humid climate of the coast was unsuitable for wine production, Phillip moved his vineyards inland where they prospered in the favorable soil and drier climate.

The British quickly recognized the possibilities for large-scale production of wines in Australia, and by the mid-1800s the colony's vineyards were expanding rapidly. Immigrants from France, Italy, and Germany helped fuel the colony's rapid growth with their thorough knowledge of viticulture. The region became most well known for its production of sweet, fortified wines, which were preferred by the British during this era. By 1900, Great Britain imported over half a million gallons of wine per year from Australia, and the continent seemed poised for international success.

Unfortunately, the wine industry tends to move in a cyclical manner, and Australia was no exception. From the early 1900s through the end of World War II, the continent's winegrowers experienced a series of droughts, outbreaks of phylloxera, and economic woes. Even following the war, when world conditions supported the export of wines, Australia's vast supply of fortified wines was met with little demand abroad. Tastes had shifted, with consumers desiring lighter table varieties, and the majority of Australia's wine continued to be sold domestically. Indeed, in 1980, nearly 99 percent of all Australian wine was consumed within the country.

In the late 1960s and early 1970s, the Australian wine industry, recognizing a need to modernize to compete on an international scale, invested heavily in wine production technology. Additionally, a system of wine ratings and reviews, the Wine Show System, began to enforce high-quality standards on Australian wines. As a result of this determined effort, exports now represent nearly 40 percent of Australia's wine production, and this number continues to increase rapidly. Today, Australian wines are known for their good quality and especially for their affordability, with high-volume producers selling well-known brands throughout the world. Its wines have permeated nearly every level of wine drinking, from high-end connoisseur's events to the daily household shopping list.

Southeastern Australia: New South Wales

The origin of Australian wine production, New South Wales continues to be one of the most important wine regions in the country. This state contains a wide variety of climate zones, geologic formations, and soil types. Close to Sydney and the Pacific Ocean, the Hunter area boasts many of the region's most well-known wineries and is a popular destination for tourists. To the west, across the Great Dividing Range, the zones of Mudgee and Orange have become known for their Cabernets and Chardonnays grown in a drier climate. Farther to the west, Riverina produces vast quantities of grapes, mostly used to produce inexpensive wines. Throughout New South Wales, the most popular wine varietals are Shiraz (also referred to as Hermitage in Australia), Cabernet Sauvignon, Chardonnay, and Sémillon.

Wine production in New South Wales followed the history of the country as a whole, with strong growth led by British monopolization of the industry in the nineteenth century and then a recession and series of droughts and diseases in the first half of the twentieth. Following the country's resurgence in the late 1960s and early 1970s, New South Wales emerged as Australia's continuing leader of viticulture.

Mudgee

Only recently changing its reputation for producing low-quality wine, Mudgee has earned itself a name for its powerful Shiraz and Cabernet Sauvignon varietals. Vineyards are planted in the hills around the Great Dividing Range, and large portions of the grapes are sent to the Hunter region to produce a finished product.

The climate in Mudgee is warm. Vineyards are planted on the hilly terrain, from around 1,500 to 2,000 feet in altitude, and the soil consists of a mixture of quartz, gravel, and red volcanic material with some occasional limestone. This fertile mix makes vines grow quickly, and a level of restraint is necessary to produce quality grapes.

The important varieties of the region include Cabernet Sauvignon, Shiraz, Chardonnay, and Sémillon, each of which takes on specific characters when produced in the region. The Cabernet Sauvignon grows quite full-bodied due to the late harvest and generally has flavors of blackberry, and tannins. Shiraz, the dominant variety in Mudgee, holds an earthy yet powerful taste. The hot days and cold nights give Mudgee Chardonnay fig and peach tastes, and later-harvested Mudgee Sémillon produces a full, lush wine.

The Hunter Valley

Encompassing the lower and upper Hunter Valleys, this finicky wine region somehow produces many of Australia's fine wines. The lower valley is humid and hot, while the upper requires irrigation to combat its dry climate, yet the region manages to retain and build upon its quality reputation. The Hunter Valley imports a significant proportion of the grapes used for its wine production, which explains why an area not particularly suited to viticulture still produces great wine. Chardonnay, Sémillon, Shiraz, Merlot, and Cabernet Sauvignon are particularly good.

The Hunter Valley's climate is not conducive to viticulture. Hot summers and cool winters, combined with frequent droughts, dumping rain, hail, and thunderstorms, make growing wine here a constant challenge. Diseases, rot, and lack of water all pose serious threats. Most wines are grown on flat, low-lying plains, but vineyards have expanded onto steeper slopes as well. Wine is grown at altitudes of up to 2,000 feet, with the majority of the high-altitude wines coming from the Brokenback Range in the west. The soil type varies throughout the region. The flatter regions drain well due to the high quantities of sand and silt, while the mountainous soil contains red gravel, basalt, and granite.

The Hunter Valley produces Cabernet Sauvignon and Merlot but is best known for its rich and nutty Chardonnay, earthy and dense Shiraz, and particularly its crisp, distinctive Sémillon. Since the Hunter Valley is roughly two hours north of Sydney, comparable to Napa Valley's distance from San Francisco, can you blame the Aussies for braving all and producing wine there?

Western Australia

In contrast to the vast geographical size of the state, Western Australia produces only 6 percent of Australia's wine, with the vine-growing region exclusively concentrated in the southwest corner. Though vines were first cultivated in this state in the early 1800s, Western Australia's wine district remained insignificant until the 1970s. Even with substantial investment, the wineries of this region still remain mostly small and family owned. As a result, the region has become quite well known for its boutique, limited-production wines. Red wines, specifically Cabernet, Shiraz, and Pinot Noir, make up the area's best-known varietals.

Margaret River

A recent development in the Western Australian wine world, Margaret River produces top-quality Sauvignon Blanc, Chardonnay, Sémillon, Cabernet Sauvignon, and Shiraz. Vineyards are grown on rolling hills in a warm climate tempered by the region's proximity to the Indian Ocean.

Margaret River lies near the coast well south of the state capital of Perth, where the cool ocean keeps the climate mild throughout the year, and diurnal variation is minimal. Rainfall is abundant, falling mostly during the winter. Vineyards grow along the Margaret River Valley and creep up the hillsides along its edge. Slopes are generally gradual to flat.

Although the soil in this region varies from quite fertile inland to less favorable near the coast, both zones are good for wine production. In these areas, Margaret River excels at Chardonnay and produces a fruity Sémillon, a herbaceous Sauvignon Blanc, an elegant Cabernet Sauvignon, and a subtle Shiraz.

Swan District

Just north of the state capital of Perth, Swan District, or Swan Valley, is a hotspot of wine production. Even with the highest temperatures of any wine region in Western Australia, the region still produces excellent fortified wines as well as Cabernet Sauvignon and Shiraz.

The slightly Mediterranean climate results in early harvests, which in turn lead to less flavorful wines. The area is composed of flat terrain, expanding marginally into the surrounding hills, and the soil is alluvial, sandy, or gravelly, and drains well.

The three most important varieties of the region are the rich and popular Chenin Blanc, Verdelho, which excels in the hot and dry Swan District, and the savory and earthy Shiraz.

Victoria and Tasmania

Once the largest wine producer in Australia, Victoria now matches New South Wales in producing a significant portion of Australia's wine. With a vast variety of climate zones and terroir, Victoria also boasts an extremely wide variety of wine production, ranging from powerful Cabernet and Shiraz to elegant Pinot Noir to decadent dessert wines of the highest quality.

The state of Victoria is divided into several wine-producing regions: temperate Yarra Valley and Geelong in the south near Melbourne, warmer Bendigo and Heathcote in the central zone, Rutherglen and Alpine Valley even farther north, and the Pyrenees area to the west. Tasmania, a recent addition to Australia's wine exploits, produces varieties of top quality in a beautiful natural environment.

Yarra Valley

One of the top wine-producing regions in all of Australia, the Yarra Valley has been compared to France's Burgundy region. Bolstered by a cool climate, long growing season, and loamy, volcanic soil, winemakers in this zone produce world-class Pinot Noir, Merlot, Shiraz, and sparkling wines. Now a major wine region, Yarra Valley produces both boutique wines and mass-marketed brands and has gained a serious reputation for wine.

Located just northeast of the city of Melbourne, Yarra Valley has a cool climate, with wet winters and springs and dry summers. Spring rains can be unpredictable, so annual harvests vary extensively. Most of the vineyards lie within the valley at just over 100 feet of altitude, though some climb to 1,200 feet. The loamy, volcanic soil provides a fairly fertile base for Yarra's vineyards. These vineyards produce a sophisticated Chardonnay, a fruitful Sauvignon Blanc, an elegant Pinot Noir, a heavy Cabernet Sauvignon, and a variety of sparkling wines developed through foreign investment

Tasmania

Growing less than half a percent of Australia's total wine crop, the island of Tasmania nonetheless remains undaunted by the large continental producers. In its temperate climate and rocky soil, winemakers have succeeded with Pinot Gris, Gewürztraminer, Riesling, and Chardonnay.

This island, located south of the state of Victoria, has a cool climate similar to that of Alsace in France. Diurnal variation is minimal, and temperatures remain similar year round because of the effect of the surrounding ocean. Despite the cool temperatures, rain is rare, making irrigation a necessity throughout much of the island's vineyards. Spring and fall frosts are not uncommon, and winemakers must take precautions to avoid losing their crops. Most vineyards grow on moderately sloping hills, enabling the cold air to sink into the valleys below. The rocky soil provides good drainage for the Pinot Gris, Gewürztraminer, Riesling, Chardonnay, and Pinot Noir. The lemony and acidic Riesling benefits from the cool climate, as does the subtle Chardonnay. Pinot Gris, Tasmania's most famous variety, is nutty and soft. Pinot Noir is the only red grown in Tasmania. Sparkling wines benefit from the cool climates, which create high-flavor, low-sugar varieties.

South Australia

The state encompasses an extremely diverse and productive wine-growing area, known for vast quantities of inexpensive wines, but it is also famous for some of the best high-quality production zones in the country. Much of the inland areas crank out millions of gallons of bulk wine, while subregions such as Adelaide Hills, Barossa Valley, and Coonawarra produce coveted, top-quality wines that stand out in any level of competition. The state is particularly famous for its *terra rossa* ("red earth") soil, which produces excellent red varietals in the Limestone Coast region. Overall, South Australia is responsible for nearly 50 percent of Australia's wine.

Coonawarra

To many, Coonawarra produces the finest wines on the Australian continent, especially Cabernet Sauvignon and Shiraz. Much farther south than Adelaide Hills or Barossa Valley, Coonawarra lies in the Limestone Coast area of South Australia and enjoys a mild Mediterranean climate. Famous for its terra rossa soil, the region also contains areas of black soil that are equally suited to the cultivation of top-quality vineyards. Vineyards grow across rolling hills and plains of the region, which owes its magnificent success in part to its climate but mostly to the soil. As a result, grapes are small and concentrated, resulting in intense flavors.

Reds dominate the region, with a tempered Shiraz, a Merlot normally blended with other grapes, and the intense Cabernet Sauvignon—the best produced in Australia.

Barossa Valley

A South Australian classic, Barossa Valley has gained international fame for its bold red wines. It's also the oldest wine production region in South Australia. The vineyards of Barossa Valley are mostly irrigated on the hot, flat valley floor, while a few cooler-climate varietals grow higher in the hills surrounding the region.

Barossa Valley basks in a hot and dry inland climate. Summers are very warm, and winters are only moderately wet. Fruit is harvested at night to avoid the heat and oxidation of the grape juice. Vineyards have been planted mostly in the valley itself, with a few outliers nestled among the surrounding hills. The Barossa Valley soil is composed of sand, loam, and silt lying over a subsoil of clay. The region produces an alcoholic Cabernet Sauvignon with blackberry and dry tannins, a fruity and spicy Grenache, and a full-bodied Sémillon and Shiraz.

McLaren Vale

Along with Barossa Valley, McLaren Vale represents the core of South Australia's dynamic red wine region. Shiraz, Cabernet Sauvignon, and Grenache all thrive in the warm-weather region with low rainfall. Soils in McLaren Vale vary, with most being either sandy or clay based. The sandy soil drains particularly well and has a low concentration of nutrients. As a result, vines must search hard for nourishment. Combined with the dry climate, this creates a stressful region for the plants, leading them to produce extremely concentrated and flavorful grapes.

Shiraz makes up 60 percent of the red varietals grown in the region, and this rich and intense wine is incredibly ripe and jammy. The region also produces a big, fruity, and spicy Grenache, a soft and smooth Chardonnay, and a pleasant, soft, and ripe Cabernet Sauvignon.

Adelaide Hills

This coastal region of South Australia produces grapes of high quality in its cool, Mediterranean climate. Elevation and soil types vary extensively throughout, but most vineyards are grown on medium-sloped hills in a red loam soil. The region makes excellent Chardonnay, Pinot Noir, and Riesling.

Adelaide Hills' vineyards are grown on sloping terrain at altitudes of 1,000 to 2,200 feet on the famous terra rossa over a substrate of limestone.

Best known for its subtle, elegant Pinot Noir, Adelaide Hills also produces Chardonnay, sparkling wine, a grassy Sauvignon Blanc that tastes of gooseberries and tropical fruits (arguably the best produced in Australia), and a Cabernet Sauvignon with solid tannins and a red berry and mint taste.

NEW ZEALAND

Key Tastes

Sauvignon Blanc, Chardonnay, Pinot Noir, Bordeaux blends, Syrah

Sauvignon Blanc has piercing aromas and crisp acidity, and in New Zealand's Marlborough region, it is particularly grassy and tropical. New Zealand Pinot Noir, rarely blended, has notes of berries, low tannin, and medium acidity. The Chardonnay is full-flavored, easy drinking, and hardly ever sharp or aggressive, and in New World can be bigger bodied, smooth, and buttery.

New Zealand Syrah creates bold, peppery wines. New Zealand's take on Bordeaux blends contain the following wines: Cabernet Sauvignon, Merlot, Cabernet Franc, Malbec, or Petit Verdot.

When people think of New Zealand's wine, they tend to conflate it with Australia's. Nothing could be further from the truth. Winemaking in New Zealand developed at a much slower pace than in its western neighbor, and New Zealand still musters only a tiny fraction of what the giant Australia can produce. But all that began to change in the 1970s, and New Zealand's wine industry has absolutely exploded in the last fifteen years. Today New Zealand exports two-thirds of its wine and is quickly making a name for itself on the world scene. In particular, its Marlborough Sauvignon Blancs have garnered international recognition for their grassy and herbal aromas and grapefruit tang, and its velvety Pinot Noirs from Central Otago further catapulted New Zealand wines onto the global map. Gone are the days when New Zealand and Australia were lumped together into a single wine region. Today New Zealand's premier wines can stand shoulder to shoulder with the best of France or California.

The winemaking industry in New Zealand may have begun in 1819, when the first vines were planted on North Island. It may have begun in 1836, when an Australian winemaker made New Zealand's first wine. Or it may have begun in 1873, when the country produced its first wine for commercial purposes. Regardless of its exact origin, winemaking in New Zealand was extraordinarily slow to develop.

When phylloxera devastated the country's vines at the end of the nineteenth century, New Zealand approached the problem differently than other countries. Instead of grafting their own vines onto American rootstock, they simply planted American vines and used American grapes to produce New Zealand wine. In addition, New Zealand growers were permitted to add both sugar and water to wines to increase volume and compensate for underripe grapes. The combination of American vines and questionable practices produced wine of such poor quality that for much of the twentieth century most of the wine drunk in New Zealand was actually imported from Australia.

The situation began to improve in the 1970s when growers started to place a greater emphasis on quality. Hardy grapes were replaced with superior vinifera varieties, and the government finally put limits on the amount of water that growers could add to wine. Local interest and government subsidies led to an explosion of production, and exports soon became a major market.

Today, New Zealand's wine industry is thriving. New Zealand produces primarily Sauvignon Blanc, Chardonnay, Pinot Noir, and Bordeaux blends.

Marlborough

Pick a spot in the Wairu Plains and look toward the horizon; you'll see nothing but vines in every direction. You're standing in the heartland of Marlborough, New Zealand's largest and best-known wine district. It's young, it's hot, and its reputation is only getting better.

Marlborough's fame is built upon its Sauvignon Blanc, which is known for its intense flavor; its aromas of grass, herbs, and gooseberries; and its grapefruit edge. In addition to Sauvignon Blanc, Marlborough grows large amounts of early ripening Chardonnay and Pinot Noir. In recent years it has added to its variety and begun production of *méthode champenoise* sparkling wines.

The sharp drop in nighttime temperature makes Marlborough ideal for growing acidic grapes, like Sauvignon Blanc, and results in Marlborough's trademark tropical fruit tastes, grapefruit tang, and hints of herbs and strong grassiness.

Hawke's Bay

With a winemaking history dating to the nineteenth century, Hawke's Bay is one of New Zealand's oldest and best-known wine regions. Chardonnay is the most popular grape here, but relatively warm temperatures support

Cabernet Sauvignon and Merlot as well. In fact, the range of conditions throughout Hawke's Bay allows it to produce fine wines of a particularly Burgundian style. Due to the popularity of the wine trail, local vineyards generally offer tours, tasting, and dining facilities. Regional tours are available by coach, limousine, bicycle, or horse and cart. Jenny Dobson of Te Awa Winery is the region's most well-known winemaker, having trained extensively in France before returning to her native New Zealand. Her Sauvignon Blanc, Chardonnay, and Bordeaux-style reds are some of the best New Zealand has to offer.

There is considerable variation in Hawke's Bay, as the soil ranges from alluvial and gravelly to hard clay; from silt to loam; from stony to sandy loam over clay. The Sauvignon Blanc grown here has consistently less of the grassy or herbaceous aromas so distinctive of the Marlborough Sauvignon Blanc to the south. The warm temperatures in vineyards further inland provide favorable conditions for Cabernet Sauvignon, Cabernet Franc, and Syrah, while more coastal locations concentrate on Chardonnay. A very distinct region is Gimblett Gravels, located along the famed Gimblett Road, whose dry, shingle soil retains heat and allows late-ripening varieties like Cabernet Sauvignon to mature before the weather cools off.

Central Otago

Central Otago, the most southern wine region in the world, is full of distinctions and extremes. Cool and exceedingly dry, its production, which increased twenty-fold in the past twelve years, is composed of two-thirds Pinot Noir. Otago's overall good reputation, based on its full, supple Pinot Noir, its lean Chardonnay, and its Burgundian-style Pinot Gris, is coupled with recognition for its high prices.

Otago lies almost at the southern tip of New Zealand's South Island, and its vineyards are almost entirely inland. Despite being the coldest wine region in New Zealand, summer temperatures in the daytime can be among the hottest in New Zealand, paired with equally dramatic nights when temperatures can fall by as much as 30° Celsius. Precipitation is very low—signs outside some vineyards even go so far as to remind passersby that they are in a water-conserving desert. In general, vineyards are on warm, north-facing hillsides to ensure that the grapes get as much sun as possible. The most densely planted region so far is Bannockburn, located between Lowburn and the Cromwell Basin.

Otago produces excellent Pinot Noir without heat due to two factors: the vast amount of sunshine and the significant differences in diurnal temperature. The central question of Otago wine is how Pinot Noir grows so well with so little heat. Otago's geography ensures consistent sun during the summer, and the sparse cloud cover ensures that the sun always reaches the vines. In fact, humidity is so low that grape rot is virtually nonexistent. Secondly, ripening occurs during warm daytime hours, but cool nights preserve acidity and nourish vibrant fruit flavors. In addition, the soil in the region is schistous loess. Its heavy texture is good for Pinot grapes, and water turns it to powder rather than clay, so it provides excellent drainage.

Yearly climate variations have a large effect here, and Pinot Noir can range from grassy in cool years to fragrant and perfumed in warmer ones. In addition to Pinot Noir, the region also produces Pinot Gris and Chardonnay.

OTHER REGIONS

Auckland/Northland: small regions near the tip of New Zealand's North Island that produce Chardonnay and Merlot and a smaller amount of Cabernet Franc

Canterbury: produces a variety of wine, including Pinot Noir, Chardonnay, Sauvignon Blanc, and Riesling

Waiheke Island: forty-five minutes by ferry from Auckland, Waiheke Island has an entirely unique microclimate extremely similar to that of Bordeaux, and it is for this reason that it is producing New Zealand's top Bordeaux blend: Destiny Bay's Magna Praemia ($285/bottle in the United States!)

Gisborne: slowly beginning to concentrate on smaller production and higher quality, Gisborne mainly produces Chardonnay and Gewürztraminer

Nelson: sharing a similar climate to nearby Marlborough, Nelson's production is growing as the rising real estate prices in Marlborough make it look increasingly attractive. Pinot Noir and Chardonnay are the most popular grapes grown. Nelson is a fabulous place to visit as a tourist; many of the region's wineries offer delightful lunches overlooking the valley.

Waikato/Bay of Plenty: only twelve wineries produce mainly Chardonnay and Cabernet Sauvignon

Wairarapa: enjoys a similar climate to Marlborough's, boasts numerous small premium wineries, and produces high-quality wines, but is better known for one of its subregions, Martinborough, which is known especially for its Pinot Noir but also for its Sauvignon Blanc and Chardonnay

Glossary

ACETIC

Negatively refers to a sharp vinegar-like taste and smell. This phenomenon occurs as a result of the presence of acetobacter, a bacteria that naturally converts wine to vinegar in the presence of oxygen.

ACETIC ACID

The chief volatile acid in wine. The flavor of wine is improved by small amounts, but larger quantities result in vinegar-like qualities.

ACIDIFICATION

A process practiced in warm areas whereby a winemaker adds acid to grape must before fermentation to counter-act naturally low acid levels.

ALBARIZA

A white-surfaced, chalklike soil found in the Sherry-producing region in southern Spain. Albariza consists of large amounts of limestone mixed with clay and sand.

ALCOHOL

A colorless, volatile, flammable liquid that is the intoxicating constituent of wine, beer, spirits, and other drinks. Alcohol is also used as an industrial solvent and as fuel.

AMARONE

The most famous dried grape wine in Italy, Amarone is produced from the same grape varieties and zones as Valpolicella.

AMELIORATION

A term that means "improvement," it is a euphemism for chemical intervention in winemaking.

AMERICAN VITICULTURAL AREA (AVA)

The controlled appellation system used in the United States. Defined as a specified grape-growing region distinguished by geographical features, the boundaries of AVAs have been recognized and defined by the Alcohol and Tobacco Tax and Trade Bureau (TTB).

ANBAUGEBIET

The term for appellation or wine region in Germany. Each Anbaugebiet is divided into Bereiche, or districts. Bereiche are then broken up into Grosslagen.

APPELLATION

An official designation, based on geographical origin, for a wine.

APPELLATION D'ORIGIN CONTRÔLÉE (AOC)

The French appellation system that controls and designates wines, spirits, cheeses, and other foods of distinct geographic regions in France.

AROMA

The smell of a wine, or the smell that is derived from grapes.

AROMATIZED WINE

A wine that has been flavored by one or more aromatic substances such as anise, strawberries, orange peel, elderflowers, wormwood, quinine, or pine resin. Usually fortified, examples include Vermouth, Retsina, and Lillet.

ASSEMBLAGE

The blending of base wines to create a final cuvée, or blend. This is a crucial part of the Champagne vinification process.

ASTRINGENCY

The sensation of puckering or drying of the mouth's tissues. Puckering is a tactile response to compounds such as tannins.

BALANCE

A reference to the harmonious relationship between the acids, alcohol, tannins, and other compounds in wine.

BARRIQUE

The French word for barrel, it is used worldwide to describe any small oak cask.

BENTONITE

A type of clay that is used in the process of fining. Clay is mixed into wine for clarification. As it settles to the bottom, the clay absorbs and carries with it suspended particles.

BIODYNAMIC

A method of farming without the use of chemical sprays, synthetic sprays, or fertilizers and a minimal use of filtration, sulfur, and chaptalization. The wine is vinified with natural yeast.

BLANC DE BLANC

"White of whites," meaning that the wine is made from white grapes. For example, in Champagne, Chardonnay grapes are used.

BLANC DE NOIR

"White of blacks," describing a white wine made from black grapes, usually sparkling and often with a pinkish tint.

BODY

The impression of weight or fullness on the palate; usually the result of a combination of glycerin, alcohol, and sugar. Commonly expressed as full-bodied, medium-bodied, medium-weight, or light-bodied.

BOTRYTIS CINEREA (BOTRYTIS)

A beneficial form of botrytis bunch rot. It is a fungus commonly referred to as "noble rot" that uniquely produces flavors that harmonize with the grape flavors.

BOTTLE SICKNESS

A temporary condition characterized by muted or disjointed fruit flavors that often occurs immediately after bottling or when wines (usually fragile wines) are shaken in travel. Also called bottle shock, this can often be cured by a few days of rest.

BOUQUET

While similar to aroma, this specifically refers to characteristics developed during the aging process and is often used when evaluating the smell of an aged wine.

BRIX (ALSO KNOWN AS *BAUME*, *OECHSLE*)

A measurement of the sugar content in grapes, must, or wine. The level of brix indicates the degree of the grapes' ripeness (sugar level) at harvest.

BRUT

A relatively dry (low sugar content) Champagne or sparkling wine.

CARBONIC MACERATION

A type of fermentation in which whole bunches of uncrushed grapes are placed in a closed tank. The weight of the grapes on top crushes those at the bottom, releasing juice that ferments naturally. The juice in the uncrushed grapes ferments within the grape.

CHAMPAGNE

The northernmost wine appellation in France, which produces several styles of wine, both still and sparkling. In order to carry the Champagne AOC on a wine label, the wine must be sparkling and the grapes must be grown within the boundaries of the Champagne region.

CHAPTALIZATION

The addition of sugar to juice before, during, or before and during fermentation to boost alcohol levels in wines made from underripe grapes.

CHARMAT METHOD

An inexpensive, quick method of making sparkling wine.

CLONE

A group of vines originating from a single, individual plant.

COLD STABILIZATION

A clarification technique in which a wine's temperature is lowered to 32°F, causing the tartrates and other insoluble solids to precipitate.

COLLOIDS

Microscopic particles including solids, liquids, and gases. Colloids most often refer to large organic molecules but sometimes refer to smaller molecules such as phenolics, pigmented tannins, and tannins. Colloids contribute to a wine's viscosity. Some colloids are stripped from wine during fining for the purposes of clarification and stability.

CORKED/CORKY

Describes a wine with a musty or moldy odor and taste. Usually caused by a chemical called trichloroanisole, or TCA, which may be formed by the reaction of chlorine to corks, especially in warm, moist conditions.

CUVÉE

A blend or special lot of wine.

DECANT

Pouring wine out of its bottle into a vessel (or decanter), usually made of glass or crystal, for the purpose of aeration and removal of sediment.

DECANTER

A vessel, normally glass or crystal, into which wine is poured. The most obvious reason for decanting is to remove sediment that has formed in a bottle.

DEMI-SEC

A half-dry Champagne or sparking wine. Demi-sec sparkling wines are usually slightly sweet to medium sweet.

DENOMINAÇÃO DE ORIGEM CONTROLADA (DOC)

Portugal's controlled appellation system.

DENOMINACIÓN DE ORIGEN (DO)

Spain's controlled appellation system, established in 1926.

DENOMINACIÓN DE ORIGEN CALIFICADA (DOCA)

The highest rank in Spanish wine categorization. An extension of the DO system, designating regions that maintain high standards of production and above-average grape prices.

DENOMINAZIONE DI ORIGINE CONTROLLATA (DOC)

Italy's controlled appellation system.

DENOMINAZIONE DI ORIGINE CONTROLLATA E GARANTITA (DOCG)

An expansion of Italy's DOC laws. This category was created to recognize the finest wines in the country, similar to the DOCa in Spain.

DEVELOPED

A broad term referring to aged wine or the aroma of wine that has been aged. Developed aromas differ from primary fruit aromas in that they tend to consist of savory, earthy notes rather than young, fruity notes.

DISGORGING (DÉGORGEMENT)

The process of removing yeasty sediment after the second fermentation.

DOSAGE

In bottle-fermented sparkling wines, a small amount of wine (usually sweet) that is added back to the bottle once the yeast sediment that collects in the neck of the bottle has been removed.

DRY

Having little or no perceptible taste of sugar. Most wine tasters begin to perceive sugar at levels of 0.5 percent to 0.7 percent.

DUMB

A phase young wines undergo when their flavors and aromas are muted and undeveloped.

ENOLOGY

The science and study of winemaking, also called viniculture or oenology.

ETHYL ACETATE

A chemical substance that exists to some extent in all wines. In small doses it can be beneficial. In larger proportions it can cause wine to smell like nail polish, however (which is considered a defect).

EXTRACT

The richness and depth of concentration of fruit in a wine. While normally a positive quality, wine high in extract can also be highly tannic and potentially undesirable.

FERMENTATION

In winemaking, the process of converting sugar into alcohol and carbon dioxide through the oxygen-free metabolism of yeast.

FIELD BLEND

A vineyard that is planted with several different varieties and the grapes are harvested together to produce a single wine.

FILTRATION

The winemaking process of straining out solid particles in wine with various types of filters. It is an alternative to natural settling and speeds up the winemaking process, allowing for better control.

FINING (ALSO *COLLAGE* IN FRENCH)

The process of adding a clarifying agent to coagulate or absorb and quickly precipitate the colloids in a wine for efficient precipitation. This process results in clarification and stabilization.

FORTIFIED

Denotes a wine's alcohol content which has been increased by the addition of brandy or other neutral spirits.

GEMISCHTER SATZ

The style of vineyard and the wines produced by some vineyards in Austria that cultivate a variety of different grapes, which are gathered, crushed, processed, and bottled together to create a field blend.

GREEN HARVEST

The trimming of unripe grapes to decrease crop yields, thereby increasing the concentration of flavors in the remaining bunches.

HARMONIOUS

Well balanced, with no component obtrusive or lacking.

HOT

High-alcohol, unbalanced wines that tend to burn on the finish are called hot. Usually acceptable in Port-style wines.

ISINGLASS

A gelatinous material from the air bladders of sturgeons and other fish used in fining.

JEROBOAM

An oversized wine bottle holding the equivalent of six 750 mililiter wine bottles. In Champagne, a jeroboam holds four bottles.

LATE HARVEST

On labels, this phrase indicates that a wine was made from grapes picked later than normal and at a higher sugar level than normal.

LEES

Spent yeasty sediment remaining in a barrel or tank during and after fermentation.

LENGTH

The amount of time the sensations of taste and aroma persist after swallowing. In general, the longer the better.

LIQUEUR D'EXPÉDITION

A mixture of wine and a small amount of sugar that is added to the top of the wine in the bottle following disgorging in the production of Champagne to balance out high levels of acidity.

LOAM

A soil type that consists of sand, silt, and clay.

MARL

A sedimentary rock or soil consisting of clay and lime, formerly used as fertilizer.

MERITAGE

A term invented by California wineries for Bordeaux-style red and white blended wines. Combines *merit* with *heritage*. The term arose out of the need to name wines that didn't meet the minimum requirements for varietal labeling (such as 75 percent of the named grape variety).

METHUSELAH

An extra-large wine bottle holding six liters, the equivalent of eight standard (750 mililiter) wine bottles.

MIS EN BOUTEILLE AU DOMAINE

Wine bottled at the domain or winery rather than by a négociant.

MOUTHFEEL

A tasting term used particularly for red wines to describe the texture of a wine within the mouth. This relates to attributes such as smoothness or grittiness.

MUST

The unfermented juice of grapes extracted by crushing or pressing; grape juice in the cask or vat before it is converted into wine.

NEBUCHADNEZZAR

A giant wine bottle holding fifteen liters, the equivalent of twenty standard bottles.

NÉGOCIANT

French term for a merchant, refers to one who purchases grapes, must, or wine from a number of growers within an appellation then blends the different lots and bottles the wine under his or her own label.

NON-VINTAGE

Blended from more than one vintage, a non-vintage wine allows the vintner to maintain a house style from year to year.

NOUVEAU

A style of light, fruity, youthful red wine bottled and sold as soon as possible, mostly applying to Beaujolais.

OIDIUM

A fungal disease affecting vines caused by a powdery mildew. The fungus is *Uncinula necator*.

OXIDIZED

Wine that has been exposed too long to oxygen and has taken on a brownish color, losing its freshness and perhaps beginning to smell and taste like Sherry or old apples.

PHENOLICS/PHENOLS

Chemical compounds derived from skins, seeds, and stems. Phenols include tannin, color, and flavor compounds.

PHYLLOXERA

Tiny aphids (root lice) that attack *Vitis vinifera* roots. The disease was widespread in both Europe and California during the late nineteenth century and returned to California in the 1980s. There is no known cure at this time.

QUALITÄTSWEIN

German for "quality wine."

QUALITÄTSWEIN BESTIMMTER ANBAUGEBIETE (QBA)

The largest category of German wine that includes the lower-quality wines that meet Qualitätswein standards. These wines must come from one of Germany's thirteen wine regions and reach a minimum level of ripeness.

QUALITÄTSWEIN MIT PRÄDIKAT (QMP)

Literally translated as a "quality wine with distinction," the phrase denotes Germany's category of superior wines. This designation of wines is based on the level of ripeness of the grapes used in the wine.

RACKING

The practice of moving wine by hose from one container to another, leaving sediment behind in order to aerate or clarify.

REMUAGE

In sparkling wine production, a tedious process during which each individual bottle is rotated and tilted very slightly over time, loosening the yeast so that it settles into the neck of the bottle.

RIAS BAIXAS

Wine-producing region in Galicia, in northwestern Spain. *Rias* refers to the inlets made by the Atlantic into the coastline, and *Baixas* (bi-shas) means "among the rias."

RIPASSO

In northeast Italy's Veneto region, a traditional method of winemaking where fresh, young Valpolicella wine is placed in contact with the used lees and unpressed skins of Amarone wines after their fermentation. This process activates a second fermentation, imparting some of the sweet, raisinlike character into the young wine and adds alcohol content as well. See also *Amarone*.

RUSTIC

Describes wines made by old-fashioned methods or that taste like wines made in an earlier era

SALMANAZAR

An oversized bottle holding nine liters, the equivalent of twelve regular bottles.

STRUCTURE

The interaction of elements such as acid, tannin, glycerin, alcohol, and body as it relates to a wine's texture and mouthfeel. Usually preceded by a modifier, as in "firm structure" or "lacking in structure."

SUR LIE

Wines aged *sur lie* (French for "on the lees") are kept in contact with the dead yeast cells and are not racked or otherwise filtered. This is mainly done for whites to enrich them. (It is a normal part of fermenting red wine and so is not noted when talking about red wine production.)

TANNINS

Compounds that contribute to a wine's structure, mouthfeel, and astringency. Tannins in wine are derived from grape skins, seeds, and stems; the more contact the juice has with these elements, the more tannic the wine will be. Fining and filtration later in the process can reduce the presence of tannin in the finished product.

TARTARIC ACID

The principal acid in wine.

TASTEVIN

A small, shallow cup or saucer used by the winemaker and cellarman to monitor the maturation of a wine. Wine is poured into the shallow bowl of the tastevin to reveal the color and provide a core-to-rim comparison, which informs the winemaker as to how the wine is progressing and maturing.

TERROIR

The overall environment within which a given grape variety grows. Derived from the French word (*terre*) for earth.

TRANSFER METHOD

In sparkling wine production, a method in which sparkling wine is transferred to a pressurized tank where it is filtered, removing the yeasty sediment. Like the traditional method, a dosage is added to the wine, which is then rebottled.

TYPICITY

A winetasting term, derived from the French word *typicité*, that refers to a wine's quality of being typical to its geographic region, grape variety, and vintage year.

VARIETAL

A wine named for the dominant grape variety from which it is made, although other grape varieties may be present in the wine.

VARIETY

A vine's distinct type within one species of the genus *vitis*. Different vine varieties produce different and specific grape varieties, and the two are used interchangeably.

VINIFICATION

The practical art of transforming grapes into wine, synonymous with winemaking.

VINTNER'S QUALITY ALLIANCE (VQA)

Canada's controlled appellation system.

VISCOSITY

The extent to which a solution resists flow or movement. When tasters refer to a wine's body, they are in part evaluating a wine's viscosity.

VITICULTURE

The cultivation of grapes.

VITIS VINIFERA (VINIFERA)

Classic European winemaking species of grape; for example, Cabernet Sauvignon or Chardonnay.

VOLATILE (OR VOLATILE ACIDITY)

An excessive and undesirable amount of acidity that gives a wine a slightly sour, vinegary edge.

YEAST

Microorganisms that produce the enzymes that convert sugar to alcohol. Yeast is necessary for the fermentation of grape juice into wine.

Index